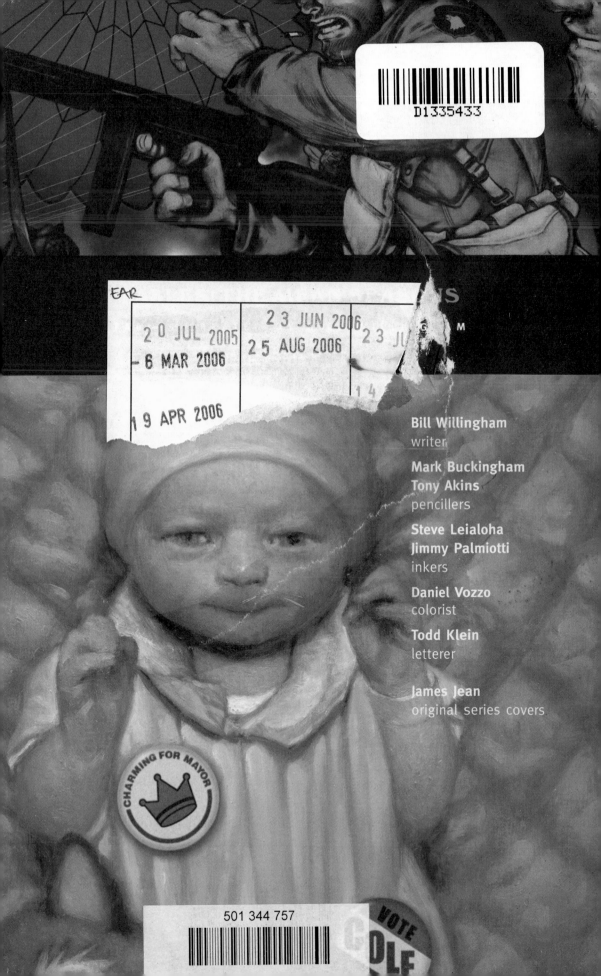

Bill Willingham
writer

Mark Buckingham
Tony Akins
pencillers

Steve Leialoha
Jimmy Palmiotti
inkers

Daniel Vozzo
colorist

Todd Klein
letterer

James Jean
original series covers

CHARMING FOR MAYOR

VOTE

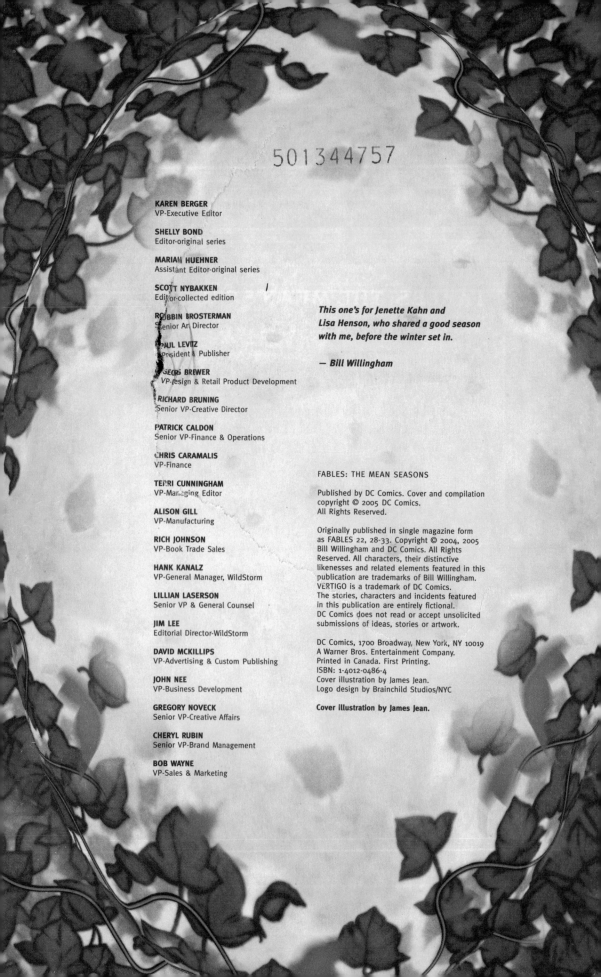

501344757

KAREN BERGER
VP-Executive Editor

SHELLY BOND
Editor-original series

MARIAH HUEHNER
Assistant Editor-original series

SCOTT NYBAKKEN
Editor-collected edition

ROBBIN BROSTERMAN
Senior Art Director

PAUL LEVITZ
President & Publisher

GEORG BREWER
VP-Design & Retail Product Development

RICHARD BRUNING
Senior VP-Creative Director

PATRICK CALDON
Senior VP-Finance & Operations

CHRIS CARAMALIS
VP-Finance

TERRI CUNNINGHAM
VP-Managing Editor

ALISON GILL
VP-Manufacturing

RICH JOHNSON
VP-Book Trade Sales

HANK KANALZ
VP-General Manager, WildStorm

LILLIAN LASERSON
Senior VP & General Counsel

JIM LEE
Editorial Director-WildStorm

DAVID MCKILLIPS
VP-Advertising & Custom Publishing

JOHN NEE
VP-Business Development

GREGORY NOVECK
Senior VP-Creative Affairs

CHERYL RUBIN
Senior VP-Brand Management

BOB WAYNE
VP-Sales & Marketing

*This one's for Jenette Kahn and
Lisa Henson, who shared a good season
with me, before the winter set in.*

— Bill Willingham

FABLES: THE MEAN SEASONS

Published by DC Comics. Cover and compilation
copyright © 2005 DC Comics.
All Rights Reserved.

Originally published in single magazine form
as FABLES 22, 28-33. Copyright © 2004, 2005
Bill Willingham and DC Comics. All Rights
Reserved. All characters, their distinctive
likenesses and related elements featured in this
publication are trademarks of Bill Willingham.
VERTIGO is a trademark of DC Comics.
The stories, characters and incidents featured
in this publication are entirely fictional.
DC Comics does not read or accept unsolicited
submissions of ideas, stories or artwork.

DC Comics, 1700 Broadway, New York, NY 10019
A Warner Bros. Entertainment Company.
Printed in Canada. First Printing.
ISBN: 1-4012-0486-4
Cover illustration by James Jean.
Logo design by Brainchild Studios/NYC

Cover illustration by James Jean.

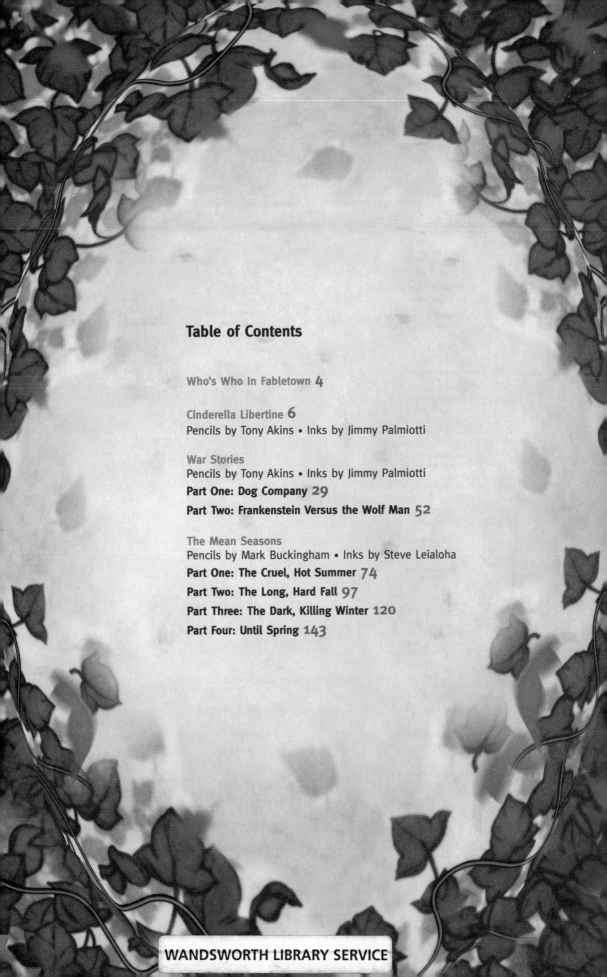

Table of Contents

WHO'S WHO IN FABLETOWN

CINDERELLA

Prince Charming's third ex-wife, and currently the owner/manager of Fabletown's Glass Slipper shoe store.

BIGBY WOLF

Fabletown's one-man (or one-wolf) police force, and the father of whatever's growing in Snow White's belly.

BRIAR ROSE

The Sleeping Beauty. She's the second of Prince Charming's ex-wives and the richest resident of Fabletown (now that Bluebeard's dead). Currently she's letting the perennial freeloader Prince Charming bunk in one of her guest rooms.

SNOW WHITE

She's the deputy mayor of Fabletown, and the first of Prince Charming's ex-wives. Since then she's remained single, so how is it she's currently very pregnant?

PRINCE CHARMING

Formerly married to Snow White, Briar Rose and Cinderella (in that order), he's single again, randy and on the prowl. But the current object of his affection is the entire Fabletown community. He's running for mayor.

KING COLE

The current mayor of Fabletown, whose job is now threatened for the first time by Prince Charming's campaign.

FRAU TOTENKINDER

Formerly the Black Forest's gingerbread house witch. Currently she's the informal leader of the 13th-floor sorcerer community at the Woodland (the main residential and administrative building of Fabletown). Recently she defeated Baba Yaga in personal combat.

THE STORY SO FAR

The Battle of Fabletown is over. At great cost, the wooden soldier invaders were soundly beaten. Now the bodies have been thrown down the witching well, and the rebuilding has begun. Life goes on. Prince Charming continues his campaign to become Fabletown's new mayor, and Snow White's just gone into labor...

BEAST

Beauty's husband. Currently he works in the Woodland's boiler room, but Prince Charming has offered him Bigby Wolf's job, should he win the coming election.

BEAUTY

Beast's wife. Currently she works in the bookstore, but Prince Charming has offered her Snow White's job, should he win the coming election.

ROSE RED

Snow White's estranged twin sister. Lately they've been getting along just a little bit better, since Rose moved away and started running the Farm (Fabletown's upstate annex for Fables who can't pass as human).

FLYCATCHER

Formerly known as the Frog Prince, he still has the occasional taste for flies. He's always getting busted for minor infractions of Fabletown law, and forced to do community service to pay for his crimes. That's why he's been the Woodland's janitor for as long as the building's existed.

BABA YAGA

She arrived in Fabletown disguised as Red Riding Hood. Then she led the Empire's wooden soldiers in an armed assault on Fabletown, until Frau Totenkinder defeated her in a magical duel. Most think she died then, but only a very few know she survived and is being held captive somewhere in the vast magical labyrinth connected to the Woodland's business office.

BOY BLUE

Snow White's assistant. He loves to blow his horn, but he hasn't been able to lately, since his fingers were burned and broken when Baba Yaga tortured him over several days.

BUFKIN

A flying monkey. Not a great flying monkey, mind you, but every story of this type needs at least one monkey and this is the best we could do. He works in the Woodland's business office, getting books down from the high shelves.

Cinderella Libertine

In which we explore something of the secret life of Prince Charming's rather outspoken and rambunctious third wife.

STOP IT, CINDY, YOU'RE EMBARRASSING SNOW.

I'M NOT EMBARRASSED. I'M **HARDLY** THE SHRINKING VIOLET EVERYONE IMAGINES ME TO BE.

I JUST DON'T SEE WHY EVERY TIME WE GET TOGETHER, PRINCE CHARMING AUTOMATICALLY BECOMES THE SINGLE **TOPIC** OF CONVERSATION.

BECAUSE HE'S THE SOLE REASON WE EVER **HAVE** THESE LUNCHES. WE'RE NOT FRIENDS-- CLOSE OR OTHERWISE. WE DON'T TRAVEL IN THE SAME SOCIAL CIRCLES.

SNOW IS IMPORTANT BECAUSE SHE RUNS FABLETOWN--WITH **MINIMAL** HELP FROM THE ACTUAL ELECTED MAYOR.

BRIAR ROSE IS IMPORTANT BECAUSE THE FILTHY RICH ARE **ALWAYS** A BREED APART.

BUT POOR CINDERELLA IS REDUCED TO BEING A LOWLY **SHOE STORE** CLERK.

NOT EXACTLY AN **ACCURATE** REPRESENTATION OF YOUR SITUATION, CINDY, SINCE YOU **OWN** THE GLASS SLIPPER, AS WELL AS RUN IT.

NEVERTHELESS, GIRLS, WE ONLY EVER COME TOGETHER ON THESE RARE OCCASIONS BECAUSE OF THE **SHITHEEL** IN QUESTION.

WE'RE LIKE AN ANNUAL MEETING OF HIS PAROLE BOARD, GETTING TOGETHER ONCE A YEAR TO CONFIRM THAT HE'S STILL AN UNREPENTANT **FUCK** AND **CONTINUES** TO BE DESERVING OF OUR ORGANIZED **CONTEMPT.**

AND IN THAT CASE HE MAY STILL HAVE *BELIEVED* HE COULD MAKE A GO AT LASTING DEVOTION.

THINGS DIDN'T WORK OUT WITH SNOW, BUT WHAT IF THAT WAS SIMPLY DUE TO NOT BEING WITH THE RIGHT *PERSON?*

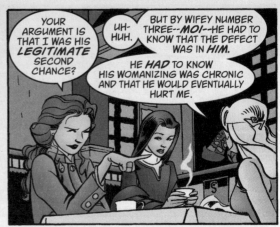

YOUR ARGUMENT IS THAT I WAS HIS *LEGITIMATE* SECOND CHANCE?

UH-HUH.

BUT BY WIFEY NUMBER THREE--*MOI*--HE HAD TO KNOW THAT THE DEFECT WAS IN *HIM.*

HE *HAD* TO KNOW HIS WOMANIZING WAS CHRONIC AND THAT HE WOULD EVENTUALLY HURT ME.

BY THE TIME IT WAS *MY* TURN, HE KNEW WELL IN ADVANCE HE'D *DESTROY* ME, AND YET HE JUST DIDN'T *GIVE* A FLYING FUCK.

Q.E.D., LADIES. I'M *DESERVEDLY* BITTER AND I PLAN TO STAY THAT WAY.

NOW, IF YOU'LL *EXCUSE* ME, AS MUCH FUN AS THIS HAS BEEN, I'M RUNNING LATE.

I'M OFF TO THE AIRPORT, FOR A WILD AND WANTON EUROPEAN VACATION.

AGAIN? YOUR SHOE STORE MUST BE DOING BETTER THAN YOU PROFESS.

ON THE *CONTRARY,* IT'S DOING RATHER SHITTILY.

I WAS NEVER CUT OUT TO BE A FUCKING *MERCHANT.*

"AND SO NOW I'M OFF TO SPEND WHAT'S LEFT OF THE COMPANY ASSETS--

Stone Soup

"BEFORE MY CREDITORS GET WIND THAT I ABSCONDED WITH THEM."

TAXI!

YES, SIR, THEY BOUGHT MY "ANGRY EX-WIFE" ACT, HOOK, LINE AND *SINKER*.

BY NOW THE GOSSIP IS ALL OVER FABLETOWN THAT NOT ONLY AM I A HORRIBLE *WOMAN*, BUT I'M A FINANCIAL *DEADBEAT* AS WELL.

Hôtel de nos Gloires Fanées

NO ONE WILL SUSPECT WHY I'M *REALLY* IN PARIS.

Hôtel de nos Gloires Fanées

I **DO** WISH YOU WOULDN'T CALL ME BY THAT NAME.

ICKY?

I DON'T **APPROVE** OF DIMINUTIVES.

BUT IT'S SO **CUTE** AND IT'S SHORT FOR--

OKAY, ICHABOD IT **IS** THEN. OR WOULD YOU PREFER MR. CRANE? OR **SIR?**

OH DEAR. PLEASE DON'T **POUT.** I DIDN'T MEAN TO--

I KNOW WE HAVE BUSINESS TO CONDUCT, BUT I DIDN'T THINK IT WAS **ALL** BUSINESS BETWEEN US.

BUT--

I **DARED** HOPE THERE WAS AT LEAST SOME HONEST AFFECTION.

THERE **IS!**

MAYBE EVEN THE *BEGINNING* OF SOMETHING ELSE.

BUT CINDERELLA, I *ADORE* YOU!

YOU *KNOW* THIS!

REALLY?

I'M POSITIVELY *ADDLED* WITH MY LOVE FOR YOU.

WHY DO YOU THINK I'M *DOING* THIS?

FOR *ME?*

DO YOU IMAGINE I'D SELL OUT FABLETOWN AND THE ENTIRE MUNDY WORLD FOR ANYTHING *LESS?*

OH MY *DARLING!*

15

AND *THEN* I'M GOING TO MAKE YOU TAKE ME OUT FOR BREAKFAST.

IS THAT WISE?

NO MORE HIDING IN THE SHADOWS FOR US.

I WANT TO SHOW MY *MAN* OFF TO THE WHOLE WIDE WORLD.

THAT IS, ASSUMING YOU DON'T MIND BEING *SEEN* WITH ME.

ARE YOU *KIDDING?*

THERE ISN'T A PLACE OR AN EVENT IN THIS *UNIVERSE* WHERE I WOULDN'T BE PROUD AS A PEACOCK TO HAVE YOU ON MY ARM.

THEN SIGN RIGHT HERE AND WE'RE IN *BUSINESS.*

WHAT'S *THIS?*

THE OFFICIAL *DOCUMENT,* GUARANTEEING THAT WHEN MY MASTER'S FORCES MOVE IN, YOU WILL BE INSTALLED AS THE IMPERIAL GOVERNOR-GENERAL OF THIS WORLD--

--WITH ALL OF THE RIGHTS, DUTIES, PRIVILEGES-- AND RICHES--THAT COME WITH IT.

WITH YOU AS MY *CONSORT?* RULING BY MY *SIDE?*

AS SOON AS YOU MAKE AN HONEST *WOMAN* OUT OF ME.

THEN LET'S GO FIND A PARSON, RIGHT *NOW!*

NOT SO *FAST,* YOU BRUTE.

IN RETURN FOR MY SERVICES TO THE EMPIRE, MY MASTER'S PROMISED ME A *HUGE* COURT WEDDING.

WITH *ALL* THE TRIMMINGS.

THE ADVERSARY HIMSELF WILL *BE* THERE?

HE'LL *PERFORM* THE CEREMONY.

BUT, ICHABOD, YOU MUST *NEVER AGAIN* CALL HIM BY THAT CRUDE AND VULGAR NAME.

HIS *LOYAL* SUBJECTS, AMONG WHOM YOU'RE NOW COUNTED, REFER TO HIM AS THE *EMPEROR*, WITH ALL PROPER RESPECT AND OBEISANCE.

BUT YOU *KNOW* HIM? YOU'VE SEEN HIM IN *PERSON?*

WHO *IS* HE? ALL OF FABLETOWN *BURNS* TO KNOW THAT--!

FORGET IT. NO MORE SECRETS UNTIL YOU *FEED* ME.

SO GO TAKE A SHOWER, STINKY, BEFORE I *STARVE* TO DEATH.

CLIK

18

IT'S DONE. HE'S SIGNED IT.

WE'LL BE OUT OF THE ROOM FOR ABOUT AN HOUR.

≈TAP≈

HURRY UP, SWEETIE.

WE NEED TO GO.

WHEN THE EMPEROR'S ARMIES COME, AND *YOU* TAKE OVER AGAIN, WE CAN TAKE SPECIAL PLEASURE IN PUTTING SOME THINGS TO RIGHT.

OH YES.

WE CAN PAY THAT *HUSSY* HER RIGHTFUL DUES-- IN A PUBLIC SQUARE, WITH A *NEW* ROPE.

NOW I WANT TO HEAR *YOUR* STORY. WHY DO YOU ALLY YOURSELF WITH THE ADVER--UHM, THE EMPEROR?

HOW LONG HAVE YOU SPIED FOR HIM?

IT'S NOT ALTOGETHER A *PLEASANT* STORY.

BUT I'VE BEEN WITH HIM ALL ALONG. SINCE BEFORE COMING TO THIS WORLD.

TELL ME. I WANT TO KNOW *EVERYTHING* ABOUT YOU.

ALL RIGHT. BUT NOT HERE.

WE'VE THOROUGHLY WALKED OFF BREAKFAST BY NOW.

LET'S GO BACK TO MY ROOM--TO OUR *BED*-- WHERE YOU CAN *HOLD* ME WHILE I TELL YOU MY TALE.

CINDY, WHAT THE **HELL** IS GOING **ON** HERE?

BIGBY'S THE MAN I WORK FOR.

YOU? YOU'RE THE ADVERSARY?

DON'T BE AN **IDIOT,** CRANE. I'M **EXACTLY** WHO YOU'VE ALWAYS KNOWN ME TO BE.

I'M LOYAL TO FABLETOWN. CINDERELLA'S LOYAL TO FABLETOWN.

THE ONLY AUTHENTIC **TRAITOR** IN THIS ROOM IS **YOU.**

YOU SOLD US OUT FOR THE STANDARD TREASON **TRIFECTA.**

MONEY, SEX AND POWER.

BUT-- --I LOVE YOU.

STOP IT, BEFORE I *PUKE.* ALL THE EVIDENCE IS IN HIS BRIEFCASE, BIGBY.

HE REVEALS OUR ESTIMATED *MILITARY* STRENGTH, AND GIVES A DETAILED NOMENCLATURE OF OUR TACTICAL MAGIC ARTIFACTS.

AND AN ANALYSIS OF OUR WEAPONS MANUFACTURING UP AT THE FARM.

AS WELL AS PERSONAL REPORTS ON EACH FABLE LIVING IN--

I KNOW. I'VE BEEN READING WHILE YOU WERE OUT.

I *ESPECIALLY* ENJOYED WHAT HE HAD TO SAY ABOUT ME.

FOR A FORMER WRITING TEACHER, HE SURE FOUND NEW WAYS TO OVERUSE "MONGREL" AND "WHIPPED CUR" IN A SINGLE RUN-ON SENTENCE.

AND THEN THERE'S THIS EXTENDED *RAPE-FANTASY* ABOUT SNOW.

NO, BIGBY, YOU DON'T **UNDERSTAND!**

IT WASN'T **ME!** IT WAS **HER!** DON'T YOU SEE?

SHE'S THE TRAITOR, AND WHEN SHE TOLD ME SHE WORKED FOR THE ADVERSARY, WELL--

--I WENT ALONG WITH IT, **STRICTLY** AS A SUBTERFUGE--

--TO **TRAP** HER INTO REVEALING HERSELF!

IT WAS A STING, BIGBY! A **STING!** I WAS INVESTIGATING CINDY!

FOR THE **GOOD** OF FABLETOWN!

HANDS **OFF,** CRANE. YOU'LL RUMPLE THE SUIT.

I WON'T STAY HERE FOR THIS **WITCH** HUNT! YOU HAVE NO **AUTHORITY** HERE!

WHACK

HE EVEN SIGNED A FULL **CONFESSION**, DISGUISED AS A CONTRACT, FOR HIS PLACE IN THE NEW REGIME.

YEAH, I'VE SEEN IT.

WHY DON'T YOU WAIT OUTSIDE, CINDY, WHILE I HAVE A PRIVATE **WORD** WITH OUR BOY HERE?

NO. LIKE YOU SAID, I HAVE NO AUTHORITY HERE.

I'LL HAVE TO LET YOU GO SOON.

DO ME A FAVOR AND LOOK OUT THE WINDOW.

SO WHAT HAPPENS NOW? WILL YOU DRAG ME IN **DIS-GRACE** BACK TO FABLETOWN?

TELL ME WHEN YOU SEE CINDERELLA APPEAR DOWN IN THE COURTYARD.

THERE SHE IS NOW.

TAXI

LET'S GO HOME. WE'RE ALL DONE HERE.

SO THERE'S NOT GOING TO BE A *TRIAL*?

IF THERE WAS I'D HAVE TO REVEAL THAT YOU *WORK* FOR ME, AND I CAN'T ALLOW THAT.

I NEED AT LEAST ONE AGENT COMPLETELY OFF THE BOOKS--THAT NO ONE KNOWS ABOUT BUT ME.

WHAT ABOUT THE BODY?

I MADE IT LOOK LIKE AN ACCIDENT--AT LEAST ENOUGH TO FOOL *FRENCH* COPS.

NOT OVERLY FOND OF THE *FRENCH*, ARE WE?

I'M NOT FOND OF ANYONE WHO MAKES *INGRATITUDE* A POINT OF NATIONAL *PRIDE*.

THEN AGAIN, THEY'RE NOT SO MUCH A NATION AS AN UNWASHED RABBLE, GLUED TOGETHER BY AN OVERABUNDANCE OF *CHEESES*.

THIS SOUNDS LIKE *REHEARSED* MATERIAL, BIGBY.

YOU'RE A GOOD CROWD. I'LL BE HERE ALL WEEK.

BE SURE TO TIP YOUR WAITRESS AND BE CAREFUL ON THE DRIVE HOME.

BIGBY, YOU OLD *HOUND* DOG!

HOW THE HELL'VE YOU *BEEN?*

COME *IN*, BOY! COME IN! DON'T STAND THERE IN THE HALL LETTING ALL MY *HEAT* OUT.

I'LL GET BEER. YOU CLOSE THE DOOR BEHIND YOU, AND THROW THE DEADBOLT. KEEP THE RIFFRAFF OUT.

THIS HAS TURNED INTO ONE PISS-POOR NEIGHBORHOOD OVER THE YEARS.

GOT IT.

HOW'VE YOU BEEN, DUFFY?

CAN'T COMPLAIN. WELL, I *CAN*, BUT I SHOULDN'T. EXCEPT FOR YOU, I'M THE LAST ONE.

YOU DON'T *COUNT*, BECAUSE YOU AIN'T RIGHTLY HUMAN AND DON'T GET NO OLDER. BUT ME...

...I OUTLASTED THE ENTIRE SQUAD.

YOU SOUND LIKE IT'S ALL OVER, DUFF.

IT IS. I GOT THE CANCER.

DUFF!

CAUGHT IT TOO LATE--YOU KNOW HOW I HATE THE MEDICOS. BUNCH OF SMUG, SANCTIMONIOUS--

WELL, ANYWAY, IT'S SPREAD TOO FAR TO DO ANYTHING ABOUT IT. I'M A GONER.

DUFF, I'M SO SORRY.

OH, PUT YOUR SAD FACE AWAY, BIGGS. MAKES YOU LOOK STUPID.

I HAD MY RUN, AND AT MY AGE SOMETHING WAS BOUND TO GET ME.

SO HOW LONG--?

--DO I HAVE? ACCORDING TO LORD HIGH AND MIGHTY DOWN AT THE V.A. HOSPITAL, JUST LONG ENOUGH TO WRAP UP MY AFFAIRS.

THAT'S WHY I CALLED YOU HERE.

HERE, TAKE THIS. IT'S *YOURS* NOW.

WHAT IS IT?

US. OUR STORY. THE WHOLE THING.

DUFFY, YOU PROMISED YOU'D NEVER WRITE ABOUT--

I SWORE I'D NEVER *PUBLISH* ANYTHING, OR *TELL* ANYONE--AND ALL THESE YEARS I KEPT MY WORD.

HELL, WHO'D *BELIEVE* ME ANYWAY?

BUT I NEVER PROMISED I WOULDN'T WRITE IT DOWN--*STRICTLY* FOR MYSELF.

AND SINCE YOU'VE STILL GOT *YOUR* SECRETS TO KEEP, I CAN'T PASS THIS ON TO ANYONE BUT YOU AND STILL CHECK OUT WITH ANY HONOR.

SO THERE YOU ARE, SON. *SIT DOWN.* READ IT.

I'LL GET MORE BEER AND AFTERWARDS YOU CAN TELL ME WHAT YOU THINK.

I'M NO SHELBY FOOTE, BUT I CAN TURN A NOT-TOO-SHABBY *PHRASE,* IF I DON'T MIND SAYING IT FOR MYSELF.

July 26th, 1944. After more than a month of getting chewed up in the hedgerows of Normandy, they promised us a full two weeks off of the front lines.

But just a few days into our R & R, they cherry-picked eight of us unlucky bastards from Dog Company — 3rd of the 605th — for a special mission.

Operation Chambermaid.

Don't bother trying to look it up. There's no surviving record. It never officially happened.

Four days later we dropped, under jet black canopies, practically in der Fuhrer's back yard.

DOG COMPANY
War Stories, Part One

Lieutenant Ronald Levine commanded us. I didn't know him too well, because he was the 3rd Platoon Leader. But he had a reputation as a good guy.

FORM ON ME.

Not a complete fuckup, like my platoon's Lt. Hilling, who should've been issued his own monogrammed body bag.

Staff Sergeant Michael Supinski was our company Top Sergeant. He was a perpetually pissed-off son of a bitch. I didn't like him.

Hell, I hated him.

But I'm sure glad someone decided to send him along.

YOU **HEARD** YOUR LIEUTENANT. HE WANTS YOU OVER THERE, SO WHY AREN'T YOU OVER THERE, ZILMER?

I'M A BIT TANGLED UP HERE, SARGE.

Private Zilmer was in the 2nd Platoon. He looked like a librarian...

TURN TO UNLOCK

PRE TO R

...but I never saw anyone who liked to fight as much as he did, after a single beer.

No shit, he even took a swing at Tice once.

I GOT MY **EYE** ON YOU, PRIVATE.

WHICH IS ALWAYS A COMFORT TO ME, SARGE.

Private First Class, Joey Tice, 4th Platoon. The human wall. He was our B.A.R. man.

Corporal John Baker, 3rd Platoon. Our medic. We called him Cutter for reasons you don't really need to know.

My buddy, Private James Schmactenberg, was the only other guy from the 1st Platoon. We called him Alphabet, for obvious reasons.

NICE NIGHT. CLEAR.

He was our sharp-shooter and could shoot the dick off a fly at 300 meters.

I guess that made up for me, who couldn't hit a barn at close range.

Private Shawn Duffy, esquire. 1st Platoon.

HOW DID A USELESS SPUD LIKE *YOU* GET PICKED FOR THIS MISSION, DUFFY?

USELESS BUT *HANDSOME*, SARGE. MAYBE THEY NEED SOMEONE TO SEDUCE VITAL INFORMATION OUT OF ALL THE PRETTY *FRAULEINS* WE MEET.

Finally there was the mysterious Sergeant Harp, the only one of us not from Dog Company. Not even from the 101st Airborne. But he knew how to jump.

We met him for the first time on the flight out here.

SECURE THE CHATTER AND LISTEN *UP.*

FOR *ONCE* THE FLYBOYS SEEM TO HAVE DROPPED US RIGHT WHERE WE'RE SUPPOSED TO BE.

It was clear right away that Sarge didn't like him. He called Harp "the man from Area F," but wouldn't explain what that meant.

But our mission was to get him wherever he wanted to go.

THERE'S A GODDAMN MIRACLE.

35

STOW IT, ZILMER.

GATHER ALL GEAR, AND PREPARE TO MOVE OUT. YOU'VE GOT FIVE MINUTES TO BURY ANYTHING WE AREN'T CARRYING WITH US. WE NEED TO RELOCATE IN CASE ANYONE *SPOTTED* US COMING DOWN HERE.

FULL LIGHT AND NOISE DISCIPLINE WILL BE IN EFFECT.

Burgstrasse

X DROP ZONE

That first night we had four hours to move only seven kilometers — the easiest walk I'd ever had since joining up.

We could have strolled. Hell, we could've low-crawled the entire distance.

Sergeant Harp led the way.

Something about him scared the frothy Irish piss out of me — the way he could move through the thick, dark undergrowth like it was a wide, empty boulevard in the brightest daylight.

He was a careful one, too.

He'd signal us to halt, just so he could point out a twig on the trail he didn't want us stepping on.

We arrived at a wooded spot in the high hills that looked exactly like every other spot we'd been humping through all night. What made this place so special, I had no idea.

The Sarge posted three of us on the perimeter and ordered the rest to hunker down and shut up.

I GUESS THIS QUALIFIES AS "SAFELY DOWN," LIEUTENANT, SO YOU CAN OPEN YOUR *SEALED* ORDERS NOW.

BREAK OUT YOUR PONCHO, SERGEANT SUPINSKI. WE NEED A LIGHT COVER.

ARE THEY INSANE?

IS THIS A *JOKE*?

AFRAID NOT.

PLENTY OF TIME TO STUDY THOSE IN DETAIL. WE'LL BE HERE FOR THE REMAINDER OF THE NIGHT.

PROBABLY THROUGH TOMORROW NIGHT AS WELL-- OR LONGER.

WHY? IT SEEMS REMOTE ENOUGH, BUT--

WE'LL WAIT FOR SOMEONE TO JOIN US--THE LAST MEMBER OF OUR DETACHMENT.

HE'S OUR *GUIDE* FROM HERE ON OUT.

MY ORDERS DON'T MENTION NOTHING ABOUT A NINTH MAN.

NO, HE'S *OFF* THE BOOKS--A FRIEND I'VE WORKED WITH BEFORE.

WITH HIM ALONG, THIS FOOL STUNT ACTUALLY HAS A *SMALL* CHANCE OF SUCCESS.

WITHOUT HIM, I WOULDN'T EVEN *ATTEMPT* IT.

I DON'T LIKE IRREGULAR SHIT LIKE THIS, SERGEANT.

WITH ALL DUE RESPECT, SIR, WHO *CARES?*

YOU COMMAND YOUR *MEN,* BUT I COMMAND *YOU.* PERHAPS YOU NEED TO REREAD YOUR INSTRUCTIONS.

NO, THEY WERE CLEAR ENOUGH-- *SERGEANT* HARP.

AS LONG AS WE UNDERSTAND EACH OTHER-- *SIR.*

So do you know what we did for the next three days? Nothing. Not a goddamn *thing* except sit on our fat asses out in the woods eating cold K-rations and keeping our heads down.

It was like a vacation. No one shot at us, and the loudest noise we heard was the birds singing.

The weather was warm, and the woods smelled like a fancy whore's boudoir — peach, cherry, almonds, magnolias and forsythias.

GOD BLESS GENERAL IKE, OR WHICHEVER OTHER REAR-ECHELON *PUKE* PICKED ME FOR THIS JOB.

IF I'D KNOWN THIS IS WHAT MISSIONS BEHIND ENEMY LINES WERE LIKE, I'D HAVE VOLUNTEERED *LONG* AGO.

Then, in the middle of the fourth day, the civilian showed up.

BIGBY!

SORRY I'M LATE, HARP. I HAD TO DIVERT A COUPLE OF NOSY *PATROLS* FROM THIS AREA.

KEEP IT DOWN. WHAT HAPPENED TO NOISE DISCI-PLINE?

DON'T WORRY, SERGEANT. NO ONE'S NEAR ENOUGH TO HEAR US.

YOU CAN'T KNOW THAT FOR CERTAIN.

ACTUALLY, HE CAN. IF *BIGBY* SAYS WE'RE OKAY...

...YOU CAN TALK, SCREAM, SING OR *YODEL* TO YOUR HEART'S CONTENT.

That night we moved out again with the civilian leading us.

‹SO WHAT HAPPENED TO YOU AFTER THE VALLOIRE JOB?›

‹DID YOU GO BACK AND KEEP YOUR PROMISE TO THAT FARM GIRL WHO HID US?›

‹NO TIME. TOO BAD, THOUGH. SHE WAS A CUTIE, WASN'T SHE?›

‹NOT EXACTLY MY TYPE.›

Most of the time he jabbered with Harp in perfect, un-accented German.

‹DULLES NEEDED ME IN LEIPZIG, TO RETIRE FIELD MARSHAL VON REICHENAU.›

‹PLANE CRASH, WASN'T IT?›

Sometimes he made us all shut up — and then we had to be real quiet.

We moved only at night and kept to the deep woods of the Odenwald hills, diverting a wide path around all villages, farms and Kraut military posts.

Our guide always knew right where they were.

Our orders were to avoid contact with the enemy.

God bless.

And the best part? Each morning, when we stopped for the day, the civilian would sneak off on his own to return in a while with all sorts of goodies.

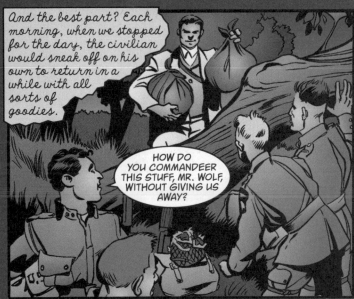

HOW DO YOU COMMANDEER THIS STUFF, MR. WOLF, WITHOUT GIVING US AWAY?

Roasted chickens, hams, meat pies, hot sausages, bread and boiled eggs. And once even beer.

THE LOCALS THINK I'M CONFISCATING IT FOR THE DISTRICT GESTAPO BOSS.

Real food and no fighting.

Why aren't all wars run this way?

WHO'D BE BRAVE ENOUGH TO CHECK UP ON ME--TO MAKE SURE THAT'S WHERE THEIR FOOD IS *REALLY* GOING?

One night our guide led us through an enemy patrol encampment. No danger, though. They were all dead.

HERE'S WHERE YOU HAVE A *DECISION* TO MAKE, LIEUTEN-ANT.

BIGBY AND I ARE GOING TO BORROW SOME JERRY UNIFORMS.

It was the most horrible thing I'd ever seen.

They looked like they'd been attacked in their sleep by wild animals.

YOU CAN HAVE YOUR MEN DO THE SAME. IT MIGHT DELAY THE COMING FIREFIGHT FOR A WHILE.

BUT, ONE WAY OR ANOTHER, BEFORE THIS IS OVER, THERE *WILL* BE A FIGHT.

AND IF WE'RE CAPTURED IN FALSE UNI-FORMS--

--NO PRISON CAMP--

--WE'LL SIMPLY BE SHOT AS SPIES.

EXACTLY.

I GUESS WE'LL STICK TO OUR OWN GEAR.

We reached our destination in the hills overlooking the village of Eberstadt.

THAT CASTLE?

THAT'S OUR TARGET, MEN.

BIGBY AND I ARE GOING TO SNOOP AROUND IN IT FOR AN HOUR OR TWO, AND THEN WE'RE GOING TO BLOW IT THE *HELL* OFF THE FACE OF THE PLANET.

YOUR PART'S SIMPLE: TO GET US THERE AND WATCH OUR BACKS WHILE WE'RE INSIDE.

UNFORTUNATELY, IT'S SURROUNDED BY A NUMBER OF *HEAVY* GUN EMPLACEMENTS, AND AT LEAST ONE MOTOR COMPANY OF ELITE SS TROOPS--PROBABLY TWO.

FUCK US.

DON'T WORRY, PRIVATE. WE'VE FOUND A WAY TO *BYPASS* MOST OF THEM.

WHICH IS WHY WE'RE HERE, ON *THIS* HILL, RATHER THAN OVER THERE, ON *THAT* ONE.

43

UNTIL LAST *WEEK* IT WAS A WORKING, THRIVING *GASTHAUS*. BUT SOME DRUNKEN LOUT OF A GUEST GOT *CARELESS* WITH HIS MATCHES.

YOU *BURNED* IT?

OOPS.

WHY?

BECAUSE I WANTED EVERYONE TO LEAVE, SO WE COULD HAVE UN-RESTRICTED *ACCESS* TO ITS BASEMENT.

FOLLOW ME, GENTLEMEN. CAREFUL WHERE YOU STEP.

I knew our sunny vacation was over when the civilian put us to work with shovels and pickaxes.

YOU'RE DOING FINE, BOYS.

A SECRET PASSAGEWAY?

AN ANCIENT *ESCAPE* TUNNEL LEADING TO THAT CASTLE ACROSS THE WAY. NO RECORD OF IT SURVIVES.

THE TROOPS OVER THERE DON'T KNOW ABOUT IT. EVEN THE GASTHAUS OWNERS NEVER KNEW IT EXISTED. YOU'D HAVE TO BE A FEW CENTURIES *OLD* TO REMEMBER IT.

WHICH *BEGS* THE QUESTION: HOW'D YOU KNOW?

SHHHHH.

TOP *SECRET*.

We entered the cramped, dark tunnel that afternoon. It was beginning to feel like a deadly mission again.

CAREFUL, MEN. IT'S A TIGHT SQUEEZE.

JUST *COZY* ENOUGH TO SERVE AS OUR COMMUNAL GRAVE?

The tunnel was about two miles long and ended in the same kind of door as the one we entered through.

WHAT NOW, SIR?

NOW WE SIT TIGHT HERE AND WAIT UNTIL WELL AFTER MIDNIGHT.

CHRIST, BIGBY, YOU JUST SHAVED AND YOU'VE *ALREADY* GOT A SHADOW.

THREE TIMES A DAY ISN'T *NEARLY* OFTEN ENOUGH.

WELL, MAKE SURE YOU SHAVE AGAIN JUST BEFORE WE GO. TRY TO LOOK LIKE A *REAL* KRAUT OFFICER.

Time crawled slowly enough for fear to well and truly build up in our guts.

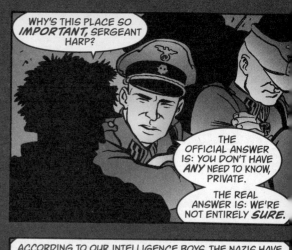

WHY'S THIS PLACE SO **IMPORTANT**, SERGEANT HARP?

THE OFFICIAL ANSWER IS: YOU DON'T HAVE **ANY** NEED TO KNOW, PRIVATE.

THE REAL ANSWER IS: WE'RE NOT ENTIRELY **SURE.**

ACCORDING TO OUR INTELLIGENCE BOYS, THE NAZIS HAVE SOME SORT OF SECRET WEAPONS-DEVELOPMENT GOING THAT MAY PROLONG THE WAR A YEAR OR **MORE.**

WE'RE HERE TO THROW A MONKEY WRENCH INTO THEIR SCHEMES.

And then, all too suddenly, it was time to go into battle.

HOLD THIS DOORWAY AT ALL COSTS, LIEUTENANT. IT'S OUR ONLY WAY OUT OF HERE.

READY TO DO THIS, CAPTAIN?

MIGHT AS WELL. I'M **TIRED** OF SITTING AROUND, COLONEL.

HERE'S THEIR ARMORY AND POWDER MAGAZINE, RIGHT WHERE IT'S SUPPOSED TO BE.

IT'LL PROVIDE MOST OF THE OOMPH FOR OUR FIREWORKS.

I'LL LEAVE YOU TO PLACE YOUR *CHARGES*, WHILE I GO ABOVE FOR A LOOK AROUND.

DON'T LET THEM *CATCH* YOU.

YOU KNOW ME WELL ENOUGH BY NOW TO KNOW THAT NO ONE WILL EVEN *SEE* ME, UNLESS I *WANT* THEM TO.

OUT IN THE WOODS, OR OPEN SPACES, SURE. BUT IN AN ENCLOSED ENVIRONMENT LIKE THIS?

I'LL BE CAREFUL, *MOMMY*.

<HEY, YOU.>

<SOLDIER.>

<HALT!>

<WHO GOES THERE?>

<KONRAD DIPPEL VON KLIEST, CAPTAIN OF THE INTERNAL SECURITY DETACHMENT.>

<PERHAPS YOU'D CARE TO *EXPLAIN* HOW I WAS ABLE TO ENTER THIS STRONGHOLD THROUGH AN *UNGUARDED* DOOR?>

<I..., UHM...I DON'T UNDERSTAND, CAPTAIN.>

<DIRECT ME TO YOUR *COMMANDER*, SO I CAN HAVE HIM PUT UP AGAINST A WALL AND *SHOT*.>

<I DON'T *KNOW* WHERE HE IS AT THIS HOUR, SIR.>

<MOST LIKELY IN HIS QUARTERS, BUT PERHAPS WITH THE *SCIENTISTS* IN THE MAIN TOWER?>

<THEY WORK LATE INTO THE NIGHT...>

<THEN I WILL SPEAK TO THEM.>

<BUT I CAN'T LET YOU GO YET, SIR, UNTIL I'VE REPORTED YOU TO MY SERGEANT.>

DEPLOY OUR B.A.R. ON THE STAIRWAY LEADING UP TO THE NEXT LEVEL, SERGEANT.

YES, SIR.

AND FIND SOME PLACE OF ADVANTAGE FOR ALPHABET.

IF THOSE TWO COME BACK ON THE *RUN*, WE WANT TO BE IN POSITION TO GIVE THEM LOTS OF COVERING FIRE.

SO, WHAT'S THE NAME OF THIS PLACE, SIR?

FRANKENSTEIN CASTLE.

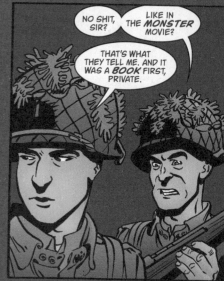

NO SHIT, SIR?

LIKE IN THE *MONSTER* MOVIE?

THAT'S WHAT THEY TELL ME. AND IT WAS A *BOOK* FIRST, PRIVATE.

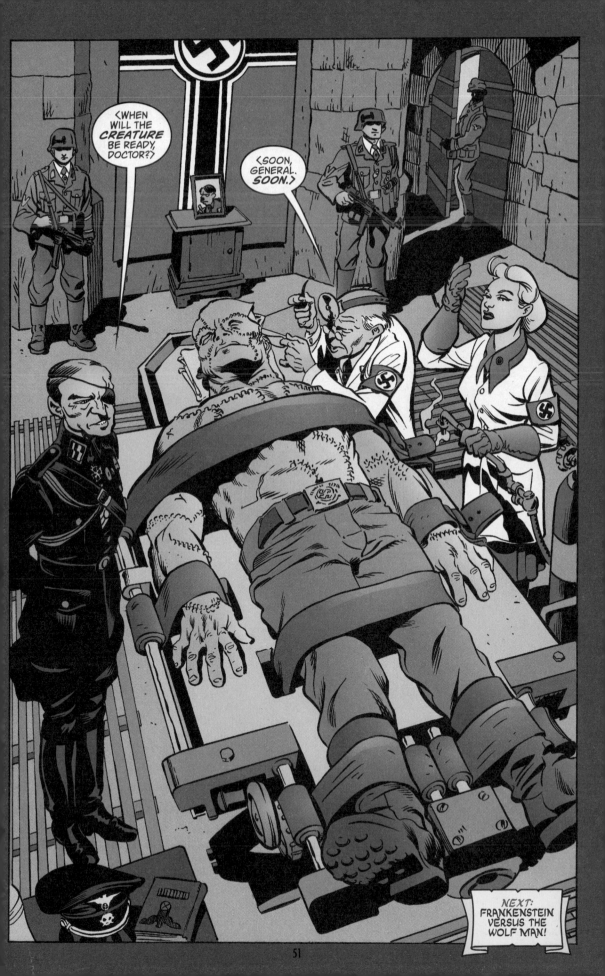

‹MASS PRODUCTION OF THE CREATURE WOULD HAVE BEEN A *MASTER-STROKE*.›

‹AN *ENDLESS* ARMY OF INDESTRUCTIBLE TROOPS FOR THE FRONT LINES.›

‹ARE YOU *CERTAIN* IT'S NOT POSSIBLE, DOCTOR?›

‹MY FATHER LED THE TEAM THAT TRIED IT IN THE LAST WAR, GENERAL. IT DIDN'T WORK THEN AND IT WON'T *NOW*.›

‹FOR BETTER OR WORSE, THE SECRETS OF DOCTOR FRANKENSTEIN'S PROCESS DIED *WITH* HIM.›

‹ALL FOR THE BEST, PERHAPS. CONSTRUCTING PATCHWORK BEINGS FROM HUMAN BODY PARTS IS ESSENTIALLY *GOLEM* CREATION.›

‹A LONGTIME PRACTICE OF THE FILTHY JEWS, YES?›

‹*HARDLY* A FIT UNDERTAKING FOR SCIENTISTS OF THE MASTER RACE.›

‹I BELIEVE OUR *PROJECT VOLSUNG* HAS A MUCH BETTER CHANCE OF SUCCESS, AND IT IS CERTAINLY MORE ARYAN IN ITS ORIGINS.›

‹ASSUMING YOUR PEOPLE HAVE BEEN ABLE TO *ACCOMPLISH* THEIR TASKS, GENERAL.›

‹WHEN WILL THE CREATURE BE READY AGAIN, DOCTOR WECHSLER?›

‹SOON, GENERAL. *SOON.*›

‹OR MAYBE *NEVER* WOULD BE A BETTER ALTERNATIVE.›

‹HOLY GOD IN *HEAVEN!*›

‹IT'S THE *AMERICAN* WEREWOLF!›

‹HE ACTUALLY *EXISTS!*›

‹STOP FIRING, YOU DAMNED *FOOLS!* NORMAL BULLETS CAN'T *HARM* HIM!›

‹I KNEW IT! I *KNEW* HE'D BE THE ONE THEY SENT!›

<RUN FOR *HELP!* SUMMON THE SPECIAL DE-TACHMENT!>

<AND THEN SEARCH THE *CASTLE!* HE WILL HAVE COME WITH *OTHER* COMMANDOS!>

<WE HAVE TO SAVE THE *CREATURE!*>

<BACK *OFF,* DOCTOR!>

<WAIT YOUR *TURN.*>

<I'LL GET TO YOU ONCE I FINISH *DISMEMBERING* THIS THING.>

<NO!>

And then the shooting started, and just like that we were all back in the war again.

HERE THEY COME!

GIVE 'EM *HELL!*

We had good positions.

DUFFY! LOB SOME *GRENADES* RIGHT IN FRONT OF THAT DOOR-WAY!

LET'S SEE IF WE CAN'T PLUG UP THEIR WAY IN.

I CAN DO THAT.

But they had us outgunned and outmanned.

CON-CENTRATE ON YOUR WORK, ALPHABET, AND I'LL KEEP THE RIFFRAFF OFF OF OUR BACKS.

ONE SHOT, ONE KILL, ZILMER.

POUR IT *INTO* THEM, BAKER!

FISH IN A BARREL, SARGE.

Basically, we knew we were screwed.

We had no idea where Sergeant Harp or that Bigby fellow had disappeared to.

<WHAT WAS--?>

JUST *ME*, SOLDIER.

SERGEANT HARP.

PFFFT
PFFFT

Inevitably it turned out bad for us.

LIEUTENANT!

But we held on.

MEDIC! *MEDIC!*

MEDIC'S *DEAD,* DUFFY!

DO YOUR BEST ON YOUR OWN!

And then, all of a sudden, Harp *appeared* again — a vengeful god of war.

But ultimately still mortal.

STOP!

〈HALT!〉

〈I COMMAND YOU!〉

〈YOU CANNOT ESCAPE--〉

〈--WOLF MAN!〉

RRRRRRRa-aaaRRGGhh!

‹I IMAGINE YOU'VE *DEDUCED* BY NOW THAT YOUR MISSION WAS A *RUSE,* CREATED BY US SPECIFICALLY TO LURE YOU HERE.›

‹DO *TELL.*›

‹OH YES, YOU'VE BECOME QUITE *FAMOUS,* SIR.›

‹THE RUMORS AND WHISPERS OF YOUR DARING *EXPLOITS* BEHIND OUR LINES HAVE SPREAD FAR AND WIDE--THE *UNSTOPPABLE* COMMANDO WOLF MAN SOWING FEAR AND PANIC AMONG OUR FORCES.›

‹SO NOW WE WILL HAVE OUR *OWN* WEREWOLVES-- A *BATTALION* OF THEM.›

‹YOUR BLOOD CONTAINS THE *LYCANTHROPIC* VIRUS.›

‹IT WILL BE A *SIMPLE* MATTER TO DEVELOP A SERUM FROM IT, WITH WHICH WE CAN INFECT OUR SELECTED SUB- JECTS.›

‹GET THIS TO MY PROCESSING LAB, *IMMEDIATELY.*›

‹YES, MA'AM.›

‹I'LL HAVE MORE FOR YOU SHORTLY.›

‹ISN'T THAT *DELICIOUS,* MR. WEREWOLF? YOU CAME HERE TO *PREVENT* US FROM MANUFACTURING AN ARMY OF CREATURE COMMANDOS, AND IN *DOING* SO HAVE PROVIDED US WITH THE MATERIAL WE NEED TO ACCOMPLISH THAT *VERY* THING.›

YEAH, FRITZ, I FIGURED OUT THE *IRONY* ALL ON MY OWN.

PFFFT

<NO! WAIT! I'M NOT A COMBATANT!>

PFFFT

<CHOOSE BETTER COMPANY *NEXT* TIME, FRAULEIN.>

<YOU SHOULD'VE KEPT MORE *GUARDS* ON HAND, GENERAL.>

<EVEN *AFTER* YOU HAD ME HELP-LESS.>

PFFFT

YOU'RE THE CAVALRY, HARP--ARRIVING IN THE *NICK* OF TIME.

CARE TO CUT ME FREE?

IN A JIFF.

CLUNK

YOU LOOK LIKE HELL.

WORSE THAN THAT. THEY GOT ME PRETTY BAD, BIGBY.

I'M DONE FOR.

NONSENSE, HARP. I'LL GET YOU OUT OF HERE AND THEN--

NO TIME, AMIGO.

WE'VE ONLY GOT *SECONDS* BEFORE THIS PLACE BLOWS UP LIKE KRAKATOA'S GRUMPIEST DAY.

I SENT THE SURVIVING BOYS BACK DOWN THE TUNNEL.

BUT THAT WAS A WHILE AGO. YOU CAN ONLY GET OUT OF HERE IF YOU MOVE YOUR ASS *NOW!*

DO ME ONE LAST FAVOR, BUDDY.

ANYTHING.

TELL *EACH* OF MY GIRLFRIENDS I MENTIONED ONLY HER AT THE END.

THERE GOES THE CASTLE-- SO I GUESS WE AC-COMPLISHED OUR MISSION.

EXCEPT THAT NO ONE *SURVIVED* WHO CAN GET US BACK TO WHERE WE BELONG.

I CAN GET YOU BACK THROUGH YOUR OWN LINES.

BIGBY! YOU'RE *ALIVE!*

YOU THREE ALL THAT MADE IT?

EXCEPT SERGEANT SUPINSKI HERE. HE BOUGHT IT KEEPING THE JERRIES FROM FOLLOWING US BACK THROUGH THE TUNNEL.

AND ALPHABET'S SHOT UP PRETTY BAD, TOO. HE'LL NEED MEDICAL HELP SOON, OR--

I CAN GET YOU BACK, AND EVEN *SAVE* YOUR WOUNDED MAN THE WALK--BUT *ONLY* IF YOU PROMISE ON YOUR *LIVES* TO KEEP A SECRET OF MINE.

WHAT SECRET?

WHAT I'M ABOUT TO *SHOW* YOU, RIGHT NOW.

AND BACK IN THE PRESENT DAY...

BUFKIN, COME DOWN HERE FOR A SECOND.

HERE'S A NEW BOOK FOR THE STACKS.

I ASSUME YOU'LL FIND THE *APPROPRIATE* PLACE TO FILE IT.

CAN DO, GAFFER WOLF.

I'M SORRY, BUDDY. WERE YOU *SLEEPING?*

YEAH, BUT THAT'S OKAY, BIGBY. I SLEEP TOO MUCH ANYWAY.

AND HOW'RE YOU DOING TODAY, FRANKIE?

NOTHING MUCH ELSE TO DO, EXCEPT WHEN FLYCATCHER, BLUE OR BUFKIN HAS TIME TO *READ* TO ME.

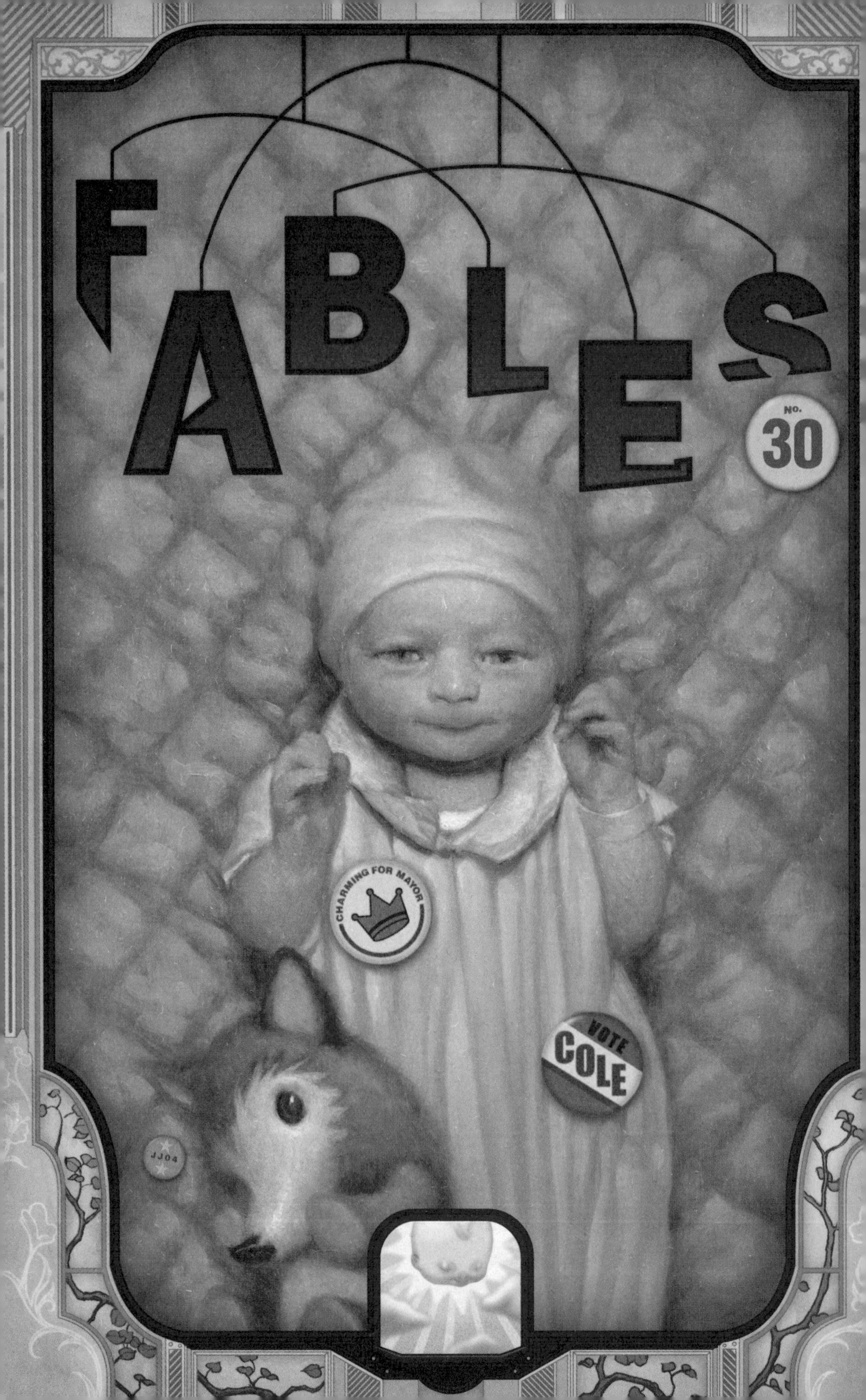
FABLES
No. 30
CHARMING FOR MAYOR
VOTE
COLE
JJ04

ONCE UPON A TIME.

STEP ON IT.

FASTER.

I'LL PAY ANY TICKETS YOU GET.

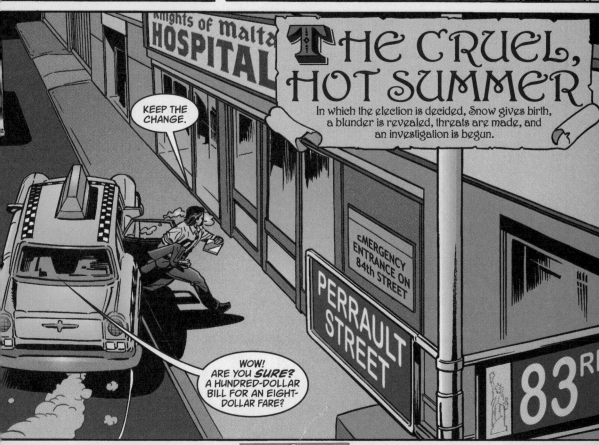

Knights of malta
HOSPITAL

KEEP THE CHANGE.

THE CRUEL, HOT SUMMER

In which the election is decided, Snow gives birth, a blunder is revealed, threats are made, and an investigation is begun.

EMERGENCY ENTRANCE ON 84th STREET

PERRAULT STREET

83RD

WOW! ARE YOU *SURE*? A HUNDRED-DOLLAR BILL FOR AN EIGHT-DOLLAR FARE?

CRAP.

EXCUSE ME?

I THOUGHT I HANDED HIM A *TWENTY.*

HANDED WHO?

NEVER MIND.

COME ON, COME ON.

MOVE.

I'M SORRY, SIR, THIS FLOOR IS *RESTRICTED* TO AUTHORIZED--

DO I LOOK LIKE A MUNDY TO *YOU,* EPHRAM?

OH, IT'S *YOU,* BIGBY. I'LL BUZZ YOU RIGHT IN.

SPECIAL RESEARCH SECTION

SECURITY

BIGBY WOLF!

WHAT HAVE I *TOLD* YOU ABOUT SMOKING IN MY HOSPITAL?

SORRY, MRS. SPRAT. FORGOT.

WON'T HAPPEN AGAIN.

SPECIAL RESEARCH SECTION

RESTRICTED ADMITTANCE

MATERNITY →

HAVE A CIGAR.

I'M BACK.

MATERNITY WAITING ROOM

WHERE'VE YOU *BEEN?* YOU'VE BEEN GONE OVER AN HOUR!

I HAD TO VOTE, CHANGE CLOTHES, AND I STOPPED OFF ON THE WAY BACK TO BUY THESE.

DELIVERY ROOM

NO ADMITTANCE

NO NEED TO ASK WHO *YOU* VOTED FOR.

HAVE A CIGAR.

THOSE ARE YOUR *CLEAN* CLOTHES?

FUNNY KID.

HOW'S SNOW? ANY UPDATE?

NO NEWS. THIRTY-SIX HOURS OF LABOR AND *COUNTING.*

WELL, I'M BACK, SO YOU CAN GO VOTE NOW.

I ALREADY DID, BEFORE COMING OVER THIS MORNING.

WHO'D YOU **VOTE** FOR?

WHO'D YOU **VOTE** FOR?

SETTLE DOWN, BOYS, BEFORE YOU START **FOAMING** AT THE MOUTH.

I **DO** WISH SNOW WOULD GET ON WITH IT. I NEED TO BE OUT AMONG MY PEOPLE-- **PROSELYTIZING** THE LAST FENCE SITTERS.

PUTTING THE FINAL TOUCHES ON MY **VICTORY** SPEECH.

DON'T COUNT YOUR **CHICKENS**, CHARMING. YOU HAVEN'T WON **ANYTHING** YET.

WHY'D YOU **CAUSE** THIS MESS IN THE FIRST PLACE? WHAT DID I EVER DO TO **YOU** THAT YOU WANT TO TAKE MY **JOB**?

NOTHING **PERSONAL,** YOUR HIGHNESS. JUST **NAKED** AMBITION ON MY PART.

AND **AVARICE.** LET'S NOT FORGET THAT.

WHY DOES EVERYTHING HAPPEN TO **ME**?

WHY'RE YOU **GRINNING** LIKE THAT, BIGBY?

AM I? I HADN'T NOTICED.

WELL, STOP IT. IT **SCARES** ME.

NO, NOT DOWN HERE, MA'AM. VOTING'S UP IN THE NINETEENTH FLOOR BALLROOM.

THIS IS THE LINE FOR *CASTING* YOUR BALLOT, ONCE YOU'VE *OBTAINED* ONE.

IF YOU DON'T YET *HAVE* AN OFFICIAL BALLOT FORM, YOU NEED TO BE IN THE *OTHER* LINE.

VOTING IS SIMPLE. CHECK *ONE* OF THE TWO BOXES NEXT TO KING COLE OR PRINCE CHARMING'S NAMES, OR WRITE IN THE CANDIDATE OF YOUR CHOICE IN THE BLANK SPACE BELOW.

DO *NOT* CHECK MORE THAN ONE BOX, OR INDICATE MORE THAN ONE CANDIDATE, OR YOUR VOTE WILL BE *INVALIDATED.*

THIS IS SO EXCITING. DEMOCRACY IN ACTION. I REALLY FEEL LIKE AN *AMERICAN,* NOW.

DO YOU HAVE ANY *BRAILLE* BALLOTS?

Vote Here

Ballot Forms

SO, FESS *UP,* FLYBOY. WHO'RE YOU VOTING FOR?

I'VE WRITTEN IN MISS WHITE'S NAME, CINDY.

HOW CAN YOU *DO* THAT, WHAT WITH ALL OF HER *TAWDRY* ADVENTURES? AND NOW HAVING A CHILD OUT OF *WEDLOCK?* SCANDALOUS!

F'ORTY-TWO HOURS OF LABOR, AND COUNTING...

OKAY, SNOW, ONE MORE BIG *PUSH!*

THE CHILD'S HEAD IS CROWNING.

OH GOD! *OH GOD!* *OH GOD!*

PUT A *GUN* TO MY HEAD AND SHOOT ME *NOW!*

I'LL *DIE* THIS TIME. I *PROMISE.*

YOU'RE DOING FINE. BIG PUSH NOW. ONE MORE.

HERE WE GO!

LOOK AT THAT, SNOW!

YOU'VE GOT A HEALTHY BABY GIRL! ENTIRE-LY *NORMAL-*LOOKING.

NORMAL? ARE YOU *BLIND?* SHE'S GOT A *TAIL!*

That's the **umbilical**. We're going to cut that right now.

Oh, god bless! Can I hold her for a minute before I drop into a nice restful **coma**?

I'm afraid not. We've still got some more **work** to do.

The next baby's coming right now.

Next baby? I'm having twins?

How could you wait until **now** to tell me?

Because I didn't know. The extremely magical **nature** of your pregnancy played royal **havoc** with my sonogram and other diagnostic equipment.

And, judging by the continued degree of **stomach** distension, we might want to plan on more than just the **two** of--

Triplets?

Or more.

A litter?

I'm having a **litter**?

Okay, you want to give me a nice push, now.

THIS LINE IS FOR FABLES *WITH* BALLOTS ONLY.

IF YOU DON'T YET *HAVE* YOUR BALLOT, YOU NEED TO BE IN THE *OTHER* LINE.

IF YOU HAVEN'T GOT OPPOSABLE *THUMBS*, OR ARE OTHERWISE UNABLE TO FILL IN YOUR *OWN* BALLOT, IT IS UP TO YOU TO *DESIGNATE* SOMEONE TO FILL IT IN FOR YOU, IN YOUR PRESENCE AND UNDER YOUR DIRECTION.

WHEN YOU GET UP HERE, YOU MUST *VERBALLY* STATE: "THIS IS MY BALLOT, FILLED OUT TO MY SATISFACTION," BEFORE DROPPING IT INTO THE BOX.

Vote Here

Ballot Forms

FESS *UP*, DONNY. WHO'D YOU PICK?

TELL ME, TELL ME, TELL ME QUICK.

DID YOU VOTE TO LET PRINCE CHARMING IN?

NOT BY THE HAIR OF MY CHINNY-CHIN-CHIN.

SURELY YOU DON'T THINK KING COLE CAN WIN?

FORTY-FOUR HOURS OF LABOR, AND COUNTING...

OKAY, SNOW, I'M *PRETTY* SURE THIS IS THE LAST ONE.

YOU SAID THAT THE *LAST* TIME, AND THE TIME BEFORE THAT!

PLEASE, PLEASE, *PLEASE* JUST MAKE THEM STOP COMING OUT OF ME!

NOW, NOW. WE'RE NEARLY DONE.

I'LL DO *ANY-THING!*

I'LL GIVE YOU THE KEY TO ANY ONE OF BLUE-BEARD'S *TREASURE* ROOMS. YOUR CHOICE!

NUMBER SIX.

WHAT'S THAT, BIGBY? WOW, YOU LOOK--IS ANYTHING THE MATTER?

I CAN HEAR SNOW. SHE'S IN A *LOT* OF PAIN.

AND AT THE ABSOLUTE END OF HER ENDUR-ANCE.

THIS IS A *GLORIOUS* DAY.

THIS IS A *TRAGIC* DAY.

TRUSTY JOHN?

ARE YOU OKAY?

OH, FLYCATCHER. I DIDN'T *SEE* YOU.

YES, MY SHOULDER WOUND HAS RECOVERED WELL. THANK YOU *DEARLY* FOR ASK-ING.

UH... I WAS ACTUALLY ASKING ABOUT--

YOUR GARDEN IS IN SUCH BAD SHAPE.

THE WORK OF A *LIFETIME*, FLY--GONE, JUST LIKE THAT.

THE BUILDINGS CAN BE REPAIRED RELATIVELY QUICKLY, SON. BUT IT WILL TAKE YEARS--*DECADES*--TO RESTORE MY GARDEN TO ITS FORMER STATE.

I'M SO SORRY.

HE'LL BE *IMPOSSIBLE* TO LIVE WITH NOW, CINDY.

WHICH YOU NO LONGER *HAVE* TO DO. MY BET IS HE'LL BE IN THE PENTHOUSE BEDDING NAIVE FABLETOWN *GIRLS* BEFORE THE HOUR'S OUT.

YOUR HANDS ARE HEALING *NICELY*, BLUE, AFTER MY LATEST OPERATION.

TWO OR THREE MORE PROCEDURES SHOULD RE-STORE THEM TO *FULL* DEXTERITY.

YOU THINK SO, DOCTOR?

I IMAGINE THIS MUST MAKE YOU *HAPPY*, JACK. WITH A NEW *REGIME* IN POWER LEARNING THE ROPES, IT WILL CREATE MANY NEW OPPORTU-NITIES FOR YOU TO SOW YOUR *MISCHIEF*.

YOU'D *THINK* SO, WOULDN'T YOU?

BUT I THINK THIS PLACE IS NOW GOING TO HELL IN A HAND-BASKET.

WE HAD A GOOD, LONG RUN BUT FABLETOWN IS *OVER*. DONE. FINISHED.

PERHAPS SO, BUT AFTER THE *CORRUPTION* SET IN, ROME STILL TOOK FIVE HUNDRED *YEARS* TO FALL.

WE MAY HAVE SOME GOOD DAYS YET.

NOT FOR *ME*, KAY. I'M ALREADY GONE.

LOOK AT THEM, SNOW.

SIX OF THE MOST *PERFECT* CUBS ANY PAPA COULD HOPE FOR.

AND HEALTHY AS *WEEDS*.

BUT ONLY *ONE* OF THEM LOOKS COMPLETELY *HUMAN*, BIGBY.

WHO CARES? THEY'RE OURS AND WE'LL LOVE THEM *WITHOUT* RESERVATION.

THAT GOES WITHOUT SAYING. BUT HAVE YOU THOUGHT IT *THROUGH?* SINCE THEY CAN'T PASS AS MUNDY, I'LL HAVE TO MOVE TO THE FARM TO RAISE THEM.

AND YOU AREN'T *ALLOWED* THERE.

WE'RE ALREADY NEARLY AT THE *LIMIT* OF OUR ABILITY TO CRAFT SPELLS. WE CAN'T PROVIDE MANY MORE GLAMOURS AND NO NEW TRANSFORMATIONS.

WE AREN'T ABLE TO *MASS-PRODUCE* OUR WORKINGS LIKE SOME MUNDY FACTORY.

BUT...

...I PROMISED.

I KNOW.

NOW, DON'T YOU WISH YOU'D CONSULTED US *FIRST* BEFORE MAKING THAT THE CENTRAL ISSUE OF YOUR CAMPAIGN?

LOOK AT HIM--WALKING LIKE A *ZOMBIE*.

ALREADY DRUNK, NO DOUBT, BRIAR ROSE.

THE FOLLOWING MORNING...

WAS I REALLY SO *BAD* AS ALL THAT?

DAYS PASS. THE SUMMER HEAT WAVE WEARS ON.

I'M GOING TO EAT YOUR FINGERS AND YOUR TOES AND YOUR *EYES.*

AND I'LL MAKE A *STEW* OF YOUR WITHERED OLD FLESH, AND A *PUDDING* OF YOUR BRAINS.

AND GRIND YOUR *BONES* TO MAKE MY BREAD.

AND NOT JUST *YOU.* I'LL HUNT DOWN YOUR CHILDREN AND GRAND-CHILDREN AND EVEN *THEIR* CHILDREN, UNTO TWELVE GENERATIONS, AND *DEVOUR* THEM TOO.

THAT'S NICE.

WHEN I'M FREE, I'LL *RAZE* FABLETOWN AND SALT THE *EARTH* IT STOOD UPON.

YOU DO THAT.

BUT FOR NOW, LET'S GET BACK TO THE SUBJECT UNDER DISCUSSION, *SHALL* WE?

WHO IS THE *ADVERSARY?*

This is the investigative journal of Kevin Thorn, former mild-mannered reporter for a great metropolitan broadcast news bureau.

I'm writing this by hand because anything on a computer can be read by any skilled hacker. So this seems the best way to ensure only one copy will ever exist.

If you're reading this, I'm most likely dead.

Pretty dramatic, huh? But let's start at the beginning.

In Manhattan's Upper West Side, between Kipling and Anderson Streets, there is a small residential street called Bullfinch.

A little over three months ago the entire street was gutted by fire, which probably occurred during an armed gun battle, but no one seems to have noticed it.

Even the few scattered witnesses who phoned in garbled reports at the time no longer remember they ever made such reports or witnessed anything out of the ordinary.

In fact, I seem to be the only person (other than Bullfinch Street's residents, one presumes) who can recall anything at all about it.

I wonder why that is? What makes me so special?

That's just one of the many mysteries I've been investigating over the past weeks.

READY FOR YOUR WALK, GUS, OLD BOY?

THEY'RE *ADORABLE*, SNOW!

ANY NAMES PICKED OUT YET?

I'VE SUGGESTED A FEW, BUT SNOW KEEPS *VETOING* THEM.

WE'RE THINKING OF *BLOSSOM* FOR THAT ONE, BECAUSE HER RED FUR REMINDS ME OF ROSE RED.

COLE IS A GOOD NAME FOR ONE OF THE BOYS.

OR AMBROSE.

WHO DO WE KNOW NAMED AMBROSE?

ME. IT'S MY *REAL* NAME.

HEY! THAT ONE'S SITTING *UP!*

NONSENSE. THEY'RE STILL TOO YOUNG.

OH DEAR.

WHY DO YOU LEAVE ME *ALONE* IN HERE, BIGBY?

I'M NOT *BUILT* FOR SOLITUDE.

WHEN WE'RE FINISHED FOR THE NIGHT, IT WOULDN'T TAKE YOU ANY EFFORT AT ALL TO PUT ME BACK WITH MY *BROTH-ERS.*

YOU CAN GO BACK IN THE HEAD ROOM WHEN YOU'RE DONE SPILLING YOUR *GUTS*, AND NOT A SECOND BEFORE.

WHINE AND CRY ALL YOU LIKE, ARLO, BUT YOUR FATE'S *ENTIRELY* IN YOUR OWN ABSENT HANDS.

THE SOONER YOU TELL *ALL*, THE SOONER YOUR ISOLA-TION ENDS.

FINE. THEN LET'S GET *ON* WITH IT.

THE LONG, HARD FALL

In which jobs and apartments are handed off, characters are forced to begin new chapters in their lives and a severed, splintered head tells all.

WHERE WERE WE WHEN WE FINISHED YESTER-DAY?

THE GATES.

OH YEAH, THE *GATES*.

FATHER ORDERED ALL OF THE GATES TO THIS WORLD *CLOSED*, AS QUICKLY AS WE COULD FIND THEM.

HE'S PARANOID ABOUT AN *ATTACK* FROM THE MUNDY WORLD.

OR WORSE, A SECRET INFLUX OF MUNDY *TECH-NOLOGY*.

THAT WOULD PLAY *HAVOC* WITH THE DELICATE STATUS QUO.

AN EMPIRE RULED BY A MAGIC ELITE DOESN'T *NEED* MODERN WEAPONS. THAT SUDDENLY PUTS ANY LOWLY PEASANT ON THE SAME LEVEL AS ONE OF OUR TOP COMBAT WARLOCKS.

NO DRAGON'S A MATCH FOR A *FIGHTER JET*, RIGHT?

IT'S ALL ABOUT THE *GUNS*, DON'T YOU SEE?

ALL MODERN TECHNOLOGY, IN FACT, SINCE IT TENDS TO LIBERATE ONE FROM A REMOTE, CONTROLLING AUTHORITY.

GOOD MORNING, GRIMBLE. I'M SUPPOSED TO MEET SNOW IN THE BUSINESS OFFICE.

GO ON UP, MA'AM. MISS WHITE'S ALREADY THERE.

HELLO?

SNOW?

SHHHHHHH!

BEAUTY...

...YOU'LL *WAKE* THE BABIES.

I FINALLY GOT THEM PUT DOWN AFTER THEIR MORNING FEEDING.

OKAY, NOT ACTUALLY PUT *DOWN*, BUT--

THEY'RE MORE *ADORABLE* EVERY DAY.

WHEN THEY'RE *SLEEPING*, SURE.

BUT WHEN THEY'RE *AWAKE*, FLOATING OUT OF REACH, *POOPING* IN THEIR DIAPERS, OR SCREAMING THEIR *HEADS* OFF FOR DINNER--

I CAN ONLY SERVE TWO AT A TIME AND THE OTHER RAVENING BEASTS DON'T LIKE HAVING TO *WAIT* THEIR TURN.

DOES WONDERS FOR YOUR FIGURE, THOUGH. YOU'RE SO MUCH MORE *BUXOM* NOW.

I'LL BET IT IMPROVES THE HELL OUT OF YOUR *SEX* LIFE.

UHM... MAYBE WE SHOULD GET *STARTED.* I GO TO THE FARM AT THE END OF THE MONTH, AND YOU HAVE QUITE A BIT TO *LEARN* BEFORE THEN.

FIRST OF ALL, I ADVISE YOU TO KEEP BOTH BLUE AND BUFKIN ON. THEY'RE *INVALUABLE.*

BETWEEN THE TWO OF THEM, THEY KNOW WHERE EVERTHING IS AND EVERYTHING THAT NEEDS TO BE DONE TO KEEP THE DAY-TO-DAY TASKS RUNNING *SMOOTHLY.*

THAT LEAVES YOU FREE TO DEAL WITH ANY *CRISIS* THAT COMES UP AND, BELIEVE ME, THEY *DO* COME UP, WITH ALARMING FREQUENCY.

OF COURSE YOU'LL HAVE TO WORK OUT YOUR *OWN* DIVISION OF RESPONSIBILI-TIES WITH THE NEW MAYOR.

PRINCE CHARMING MIGHT WANT TO BE MORE *HANDS-ON* THAN KING COLE.

NO SCARRING. GRIP STRENGTH IS GOOD. *FULL* DIGITAL MOBILITY HAS BEEN RESTORED.

ONCE AGAIN *I'VE* ACCOMPLISHED WHAT NO OTHER SURGEON COULD DO.

I'M REALLY GRATEFUL, DOCTOR SWINEHEART.

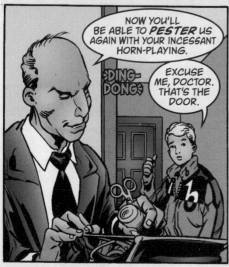

NOW YOU'LL BE ABLE TO *PESTER* US AGAIN WITH YOUR INCESSANT HORN-PLAYING.

EXCUSE ME, DOCTOR. THAT'S THE DOOR.

DING-DONG

KING COLE!

THANKS FOR LETTING ME *BUNK* WITH YOU, BLUE.

NOT AT ALL. COME IN. YOU SHOULD'VE CALLED ME TO HELP WITH YOUR BAGS.

I'LL BE OUT OF YOUR HAIR IN NO TIME.

AS SOON AS BEAUTY AND BEAST MOVE INTO SNOW'S PLACE, I GET THEIR OLD APARTMENT.

YOU'RE WELCOME FOR AS LONG AS YOU *NEED*, YOUR HONOR.

OKAY, CINDY, THAT'S ALL FOR THE DAY.

SINCE ARLO SEEMS *SUFFICIENTLY* DRAINED OF USEFUL INTEL, YOU CAN PUT HIM BACK WITH HIS BROTHERS.

FINALLY.

TOMORROW WE CAN START *FRESH* WITH ONE OF THE OTHERS.

WORKS FOR ME. MAKE SURE THAT JOURNAL GETS SAFELY *LOCKED* AWAY.

GOT IT. SEE YOU TWO IN THE EARLY *A.M.*

HOW ABOUT REGINALD? HE STRIKES ME AS BEING READY TO *TALK.*

SO WHAT'S THE *DEAL* WITH CINDERELLA? WHY'S *SHE* PART OF THIS?

SHE'S ANOTHER ONE OF THE *SECRETS* YOU'RE GOING TO HAVE TO LEARN TO KEEP ONCE YOU TAKE OVER AS SHERIFF.

I'LL FILL YOU IN ON THE DETAILS ABOUT HER ONCE I TRUST YOU'RE NOT GOING TO BE A COMPLETE *FUCKUP* IN THE JOB.

I SEE I'VE GOT MUCH MORE TO LEARN THAN I'D ORIGINALLY IMAGINED.

YOU'LL FIND OUT PRETTY *QUICKLY* IF YOU'VE GOT THE TEMPERAMENT FOR THIS JOB.

IT'S A PRETTY ECLECTIC MIX OF SMALL TOWN SHERIFF AND CLANDESTINE SPY-MASTER.

MOSTLY IT'S ABOUT LEARNING WHAT SECRETS YOU NEED TO KEEP, EVEN FROM YOUR OWN BOSSES.

YOU'LL HAVE TO CULTIVATE SOME SUBTLE JUDGMENT ON WHAT THEY SHOULD KNOW AND WHAT THEY'RE BETTER OFF *NEVER* KNOWING.

WHERE ARE WE GOING, BIGBY? THIS ISN'T THE WAY BACK TO THE BUSINESS OFFICE.

I FIGURE YOU'VE EARNED AT LEAST *SOME* CONSIDERATION.

COME WITH ME, MR. BEAST, AND I'LL SHOW YOU ONE OF THOSE *BIG* HIDDEN THINGS YOU CAN NEVER TELL ANYONE--NOT EVEN YOUR *WIFE*.

BUT SHE'S ABOUT TO BE THE DEPUTY MAYOR. MY DIRECT *SUPERIOR*.

RIGHT. THINK OF THIS AS MY TEST TO SEE IF YOU HAVE THE STRENGTH AND BACKBONE TO CARRY THOSE BURDENS YOU HAVE TO CARRY *ALONE*.

PART OF WHY FABLETOWN WORKED SO WELL IN THE PAST IS THAT I WAS WILLING TO DO ALL THE *DARK* THINGS SNOW AND KING COLE SHOULDN'T HAVE TO KNOW ABOUT, AND WOULDN'T *WANT* TO KNOW ABOUT.

HOW FABLETOWN WORKS IN THE FUTURE IS SUBSTANTIALLY UP TO *YOUR* ABILITY TO DO THE SAME.

HI, BUFKIN. EVERYONE ELSE *GONE* FOR THE NIGHT?

YEAH. SNOW TOOK HER FLOATERS HOME *HOURS* AGO.

BIGBY AND BEAST ARE STILL SOMEWHERE BACK IN THE DEEP PASSAGES.

OKAY, WELL MY NEW ROOMMATE'S SLEEPING AND I NEED TO PRACTICE MY *HORN* DOWN HERE.

SO, IF YOU WANT TO SLEEP, YOU'D BETTER TAKE YOUR BASKET TO ONE OF THE BACK ROOMS.

SURE. Y'BETCHER.

SEEYA LATER, TATER.

GOODBYE, OLD BUDDY.

TAKE *CARE* OF THESE FOLKS, OKAY?

MR. BEAST, MEET GUDRUN, THE GOOSE THAT LAYS THE *GOLDEN* EGGS.

HEY, BIGBY. HELLO, MR. BEAST.

OH MY.

BUT YOU'RE SUPPOSED TO BE *DEAD.* KILLED IN THE HOMELANDS, CENTURIES AGO.

A BIT OF FICTION BIGBY AND I COOKED UP.

WHY?

BECAUSE GUDRUN'S GOLDEN EGGS ARE HOW I *FINANCE* MY *UN-AUTHORIZED* OPERATIONS--AND HOW YOU'LL DO IT FROM NOW ON.

NEXT WEEK I'LL INTRODUCE YOU TO MY GUY DOWNTOWN, WHO CONVERTS THESE INTO UNTRACE-ABLE FUNDS FOR ME.

HOLY CRAP ON CREPES. WHAT HAVE I GOT MYSELF *INTO?*

BETTER FIGURE THAT OUT QUICK.

I'M NEARLY *GONE* AND YOU'RE ABOUT TO BE THROWN INTO THE DEEP END.

DAYS PASS.

WHERE ARE YOU GOING TO *GO*, BIGBY, WHEN THE BABIES AND I LEAVE FOR THE FARM TOMORROW?

I DON'T KNOW, BUT I'M *NOT* STAYING HERE.

I KNOW IT STINKS, BUT--

I'VE DONE MY PART, AND MORE. THAT'S ENOUGH. IT'S TIME FOR *OTHERS* TO TAKE THEIR TURN.

YOU BETTER *HOPE* NOT, SNOW. I'M GOING TO TRY TO STAY AWAY--TRY TO ABIDE BY THESE MISERABLE LAWS I'VE ENFORCED FOR TOO MANY YEARS-- BUT I DON'T KNOW HOW LONG I CAN *HOLD OUT*.

SOONER OR LATER I'M GOING TO DECIDE TO *SEE* MY CUBS, AND WHEN THAT HAPPENS, NO POWER, NO SPELL AND NO CREATURE ON EARTH IS GOING TO *STOP* ME.

BUT FABLETOWN STILL *NEEDS* YOU.

I'VE FAITHFULLY SERVED FABLETOWN FOR CENTURES. AND FOR MY TROUBLES, MY CUBS ARE BEING *BANISHED* FOREVER TO THE ONE PLACE I'M NOT ALLOWED TO GO.

WILL WE *EVER* SEE YOU AGAIN?

YOU'D TEAR DOWN *EVERYTHING* WE WORKED SO HARD FOR SO LONG TO CREATE?

WHAT WE CREATED, SNOW, ARE THOSE *KIDS* YOU'RE ABOUT TO TAKE AWAY FROM ME.

THEY'RE ALL THAT *MATTERS* NOW. ANY DUTIES I STILL HAVE BELONG SOLELY TO THEM.

THEN HOW DO WE *FIX* THIS?

EASY. DON'T GO TO THE FARM. COME AWAY WITH ME.

THERE ARE STILL FORESTS IN THIS WORLD WHERE NO ONE WILL EVER FIND US.

WE'D BE FREE TO RAISE OUR FAMILY WITHOUT INTERFERENCE FROM FABLE OR MUNDY.

OH, BIGBY, I COULDN'T POSSIBLY--

I CAN'T *BETRAY* FABLETOWN, AND I COULDN'T LIVE THAT WAY.

OF COURSE NOT. FOR ALL YOUR GRIPING ABOUT HOW ILL-USED YOU WERE, YOU STILL CLING TO YOUR *FANTASIES* OF CASTLES AND PRINCES.

WHERE *DOGS* KNOW THEIR PLACE-- IN THE KENNELS.

LET'S GO, DRIVER.

WHERE TO, MAC?

I'M NOT SURE.

LET'S START WITH AWAY.

FINALLY! THIS IS ALL **OURS**!

DON'T GET TOO HAPPY ABOUT IT, DARLING.

I SUSPECT IT'S GOING TO TURN OUT TO BE MORE OF A BURDEN THAN A BLESSING.

DON'T SPOIL THE **MOMENT**, DEAR.

HEY, WHAT'S WITH THE THIRD DESK?

THAT ONE'S **MINE**.

UNLIKE MY PREDECESSOR, I INTEND TO TAKE A MORE **DIRECT** HAND IN OUR DAY-TO-DAY AFFAIRS OF STATE.

SO WHERE'S BOY BLUE AND THAT DAMNED MONKEY? I WANT EVERYONE HERE FOR MY FIRST OFFICIAL **PEP** TALK.

WHO KNOWS? I HAVEN'T SEEN EITHER OF THEM FOR DAYS.

THINGS HAVE BEEN SO HECTIC HERE.

AUNTIE ROSE HAS *GOT* TO GET A LOOK AT HER NIECES AND NEPHEWS!

BUT--

OH, *LOOK* AT ALL OF YOU, YOU DARLINGS!

HOW YOU'VE ALL *GROWN* SINCE I SAW YOU!

GOOTCHIE GOOTCHIE *GOO!* GOOTCHIE GOOTCHIE *GOO!*

OH MY GOD, ROSE!

YOU'VE LET THEM *GET AWAY!*

WE'RE *LOSING* THEM!

YOU *WORRY* TOO MUCH, SISTER O' MINE.

WE'VE GOT IT *COVERED.*

FETCH 'EM BACK, BOYS!

OH NO! *OH NO!*

:GOOOOBBLLRR:

:BURRB:

WE'VE BEEN *PRACTICING* THESE MANEUVERS FOR WEEKS.

AMAZING!

THANK YOU! THANK YOU!

SNOW, YOU'VE JUST LANDED IN A NEST OF THE MOST EFFICIENT *BABYSITTERS* FOR YOUR UNIQUE BROOD THAT ANY MOMMY COULD EVER HOPE FOR.

COME ON INTO THE MAIN HOUSE AND TAKE A LOAD OFF. WE'VE GOT THE *VIP* ROOM ALL READY FOR YOU AND THE FLYING RUG RATS.

I'M OVERWHELMED.

THERE YOU ARE!

YOU SNUCK OUT EARLY. THE PARTY'S ONLY GETTING STARTED.

I'M EXHAUSTED. WE'VE HAD A LONG DAY.

FAIR ENOUGH. SO GIVE ME ALL THE GOSSIP. HOW DID THINGS GO WITH *BIGBY*?

DID YOU HAVE A ROMANTIC GOODBYE?

FAR FROM IT. WE HAD A FIGHT YESTERDAY AND HE DIDN'T EVEN *SPEAK* TO ME THIS MORNING.

AND NOW HE'S GONE AWAY TO WHERE NO ONE WILL BE ABLE TO FIND HIM.

COOL.

EXCUSE ME?

IF HE'S GONE OFF TO SULK IT JUST SHOWS HOW MUCH HE REALLY CARES.

OF COURSE THAT'S NO SURPRISE TO ANYONE WITH *EYES*.

YOU TWO ARE JOINED BY AN INVISIBLE CHAIN THAT NO AMOUNT OF ANGER OR DISTANCE CAN BREAK.

IT'S BEEN THERE SINCE WE FIRST *MET* THE MANGY OLD MONSTER, WAY BACK WHEN HE SPRUNG US FROM THE ADVERSARY'S CHAIN GANG.

HE ACCUSED ME OF STILL WANTING PALACES AND A HANDSOME PRINCE.

OF COURSE HE DID, BECAUSE YOU STILL *DO.*

SILLY GIRL. YOU STILL THINK THAT HAPPILY EVER AFTER CAN ONLY COME WITH REFINED INBRED PRETTY BOYS, LADIES IN WAITING AND LOTS OF NICE, EXPENSIVE THINGS.

WE BOTH KNOW HOW WELL *THAT* WORKED OUT SO FAR.

WHY NOT TRY ON A *MUTT* THIS TIME TO SEE IF YOUR LUCK IMPROVES?

IT'S TOO LATE. HE'S GONE.

FOR NOW, BUT HE'LL COME BACK.

THE GOOD ONES *ALWAYS* DO.

OKAY, SO DO THE *BAD* ONES, BUT WE DON'T NEED TO DISCUSS *MY* LOVE LIFE TONIGHT.

PRINCE CHARMING?

YOUR HONOR, YOU HAVE TO WAKE *UP.*

WHAT IS IT, HOBBES? WHAT'S THE MATTER?

THEY FOUND THE MONKEY, SIR. HE'D BEEN HIDING IN THE BACK ROOMS, BECAUSE HE THOUGHT WE'D *BLAME* HIM.

BLAME HIM FOR *WHAT?*

BOY BLUE *LEFT.* DISAPPEARED. MORE THAN A *WEEK* AGO. THE MONKEY THINKS HE WENT BACK TO THE HOMELANDS TO FIND THAT GIRL OF HIS--THE ONE BABA YAGA IMPERSONATED.

HOW?

HOW COULD HE *DO* THAT? THERE'RE NO OPEN GATES LEFT.

IT SEEMS HE DIDN'T LEAVE EMPTY-HANDED.

HE STOLE THE *WITCHING CLOAK.* ALSO THE *VORPAL SWORD* AND PINOCCHIO'S *BODY.* THEY'RE CHECKING NOW TO SEE IF ANYTHING ELSE IS MISSING.

MASTER!

MASTER!
COME QUICK!

OH BOY! OH BOY! OH BOY!

MASTER! YOU NEED TO SEE THIS!

MISTRAL, WHY ARE YOU FLYING ABOUT LIKE SOME UNCIVILIZED GUST? HAVE YOU FORGOTTEN THE BASIC COURTESY OF MY HOME?

SORRY, MASTER. I GOT OVEREXCITED BY WHAT I SAW IN THE SCRYING POOL.

AND WHAT WOULD THAT BE?

A WONDROUS THING! I FOUND YOUR SON! WELL, NOT YOUR SON EXACTLY, BUT-- OH, YOU SHOULD JUST COME AND SEE FOR YOUR- SELF!

COME ON, PEOPLE! YOU CAN'T *DO* THIS!

BUT PRINCE CHARMING *BROKE* HIS PROMISES, MR. BEAST!

ALL OF THEM!

WHERE'S THE FREE *GLAMOUR* SPELLS AND *TRANS-FORMATIONS*?

PC OUT!

NOT SO CHARMING NOW!

WAKE ME!

KEEP YOUR PROMISES!

FINE! I AGREE YOU HAVE A *RIGHT* TO COMPLAIN!

BUT *NOT* OUT IN THE STREETS, WHERE THE *MUNDYS* MIGHT SEE YOU!

OUR LAWS EXPRESSLY *FORBID* ANY PUBLIC ACTION THAT MIGHT DRAW MUNDY ATTENTION TO OUR TRUE NATURE.

YOU *KNOW* THIS!

WHAT WE *KNOW* IS THAT THE NEW MAYOR--MISTER *HIGH AND MIGHTY* HIMSELF--CAN'T BE *BOTHERED* TO SEE US!

HE'S *REFUSED* OUR ATTEMPTS TO SCHEDULE APPOINT-MENTS!

GIVE US THE

CHARMING LIAR IS STILL A LIAR!

THAT'S *NOT* BECAUSE HE'S UNWILLING TO *SEE* CITIZENS.

IT'S ONLY BECAUSE BOY BLUE IS *MISSING* AND THERE'S NO ONE HERE TO *MAKE* THE APPOINTMENTS!

E delivered e VOTES, now you deliver the SPELLS!

NOD'S BOOKS

LEWIS

Antiques NO 20

FORD LAUNDERMAT

Someday my PRINCE will GO!!!

THE DARK, KILLING WINTER

In which protests occur, magical doings are arranged, someone dies, investigations proceed, and an unexpected visitor arrives at The Farm.

BLUE *KNEW* HOW TO RUN THE BUSINESS OFFICE AND I HAVE TO CONFESS THAT THE NEW REGIME IS A BIT *LOST* WITHOUT HIM.

THINGS ARE CHAOTIC NOW, BUT THEY'LL GET *BETTER.*

WE'RE JUST HAVING A ROUGH *TRANSITION,* IS ALL.

WELL, YOU BETTER TRANSITION *FASTER,* BECAUSE *WE* AREN'T THE ONES *MOST* AFFECTED BY YOUR BOSS'S BROKEN PROMISES!

GIVE US THE SPELLS!

A CHA... ...S LIAR IS STI... A LIAR!

YEAH! WE DON'T WANT ANOTHER *ARMED REBELLION* UP AT THE *FARM!*

BUT IT'S COMING FOR DAMN *SURE* IF YOU DON'T DO *SOMETHING* PRETTY QUICK!

LOOK! I **PERSONALLY** GUARANTEE YOU'LL GET AN APPOINTMENT WITH THE MAYOR IN ANOTHER DAY OR TWO--**INDIVIDUALLY**, OR AS A **GROUP**.

BUT FOR NOW, YOU'RE IN **VIOLATION** OF FABLETOWN LAW.

Someday PRINCE GO!!!!

KEEP YOUR PROMISES!

Out!

WE deliver the VOTES, you deliver the SPELLS!

I **ORDER** YOU TO DISPERSE!

GO **HOME**, OR, WITH GREAT RELUCTANCE, I'LL BE FORCED TO START **ARRESTING** YOU!

GO **ON**, NOW.

THERE YOU GO.

THANK YOU.

NOU'S BOOKS

YOU BETTER **NOT** LET US **DOWN**, SHERIFF.

YEAH, I'VE FIGURED THAT OUT.

GRIM BUSINESS TO START THE **DAY**, EH?

DID YOU HEAR WHAT THAT FABLE **CALLED** ME, JOHN?

HE CALLED ME "**SHERIFF!**"

ME! THEY'RE BEGINNING TO **ACCEPT** ME AS THE NEW SHERIFF!

ISN'T THAT JUST TOO **COOL?**

DISTURBANCE ALL SETTLED THEN, BOSS?

FOR **NOW,** GRIMBLE. FOR NOW.

GOOD MORNING, FRAU TOTENKINDER. OFF TO THE BUSINESS OFFICE AGAIN?

YES. WALK ME THERE.

I'VE GOT **NEWS** FOR YOU.

WE'VE FINISHED THE FORENSIC EXAMINATION OF YOUR ENCHANTMENT.

AND CAN YOU **ALTER** IT?

WITH SOME EFFORT, **YES.**

SOON YOU'LL BE ABLE TO TRANSFORM **AT WILL,** BACK AND FORTH, BETWEEN BEAST AND HUMAN FORM--NO LONGER SUBJECT TO THE WHIMS OF YOUR BRIDE'S MERCURIAL MOOD.

MARVELOUS!

IT'LL BE QUITE A HELP IN MY NEW JOB.

LIKE BIGBY, WE NEED A *TOUGH CUSTOMER* FOR OUR SHERIFF--ONE WHO HAS THE OPTION OF LETTING THE *MONSTER* OUT WHEN A SITUATION GROWS DIRE.

NOW, WHILE I HAVE YOU ALONE, LET ME ASK YOU *ANOTHER* QUESTION--ON A SUBJECT I WANT YOU TO KEEP STRICTLY TO YOURSELF.

OH? SECRETS ALREADY?

I'M *INTRIGUED.*

WHAT WOULD IT TAKE FOR YOU TO GROW A PAIR OF *EYEBALLS?*

OH GOD, OH GOD, OH *GOD.*

I *HATE* THIS PLACE AND I HATE MY *JOB!*

HOW DID SHE DO IT?

HOW DID SNOW RUN THINGS SO EFFICIENTLY AND KEEP THINGS SO TIDY?

WELL, BEAUTY--

--SHE WAS PART OF THE GOVERNMENT SINCE BEFORE FABLETOWN WAS ESTABLISHED-- BACK WHEN THEY HAD DOZENS OF PEOPLE RUNNING THIS PLACE.

SHE HAD CENTURIES TO LEARN THE ROPES, AS SHE WORKED HER WAY UP TO THE TOP POSITION.

SHOULD I STOP TALKING NOW?

GO FIND A DICTIONARY AND LOOK UP THE WORD "RHETORICAL QUESTION."

THAT'S TWO WORDS.

FLY AWAY, MONKEY!

I'M GONE!

YOU'RE NEVER GOING TO GET YOUR WORK DONE IF YOU KEEP FIGHTING WITH THAT DAMNED *MONKEY* EVERY DAY.

SHUT *UP*, MR. MAYOR. OR BETTER YET, *FIRE* ME FOR INSUBORDINATION.

GOD, YES, *PLEASE* DO THAT.

THANK YOU FOR THE *ESCORT*, MR. BEAST. YOU'RE A GENTLEMAN.

GOING BACK INTO THE *DEPTHS* AGAIN, MA'AM?

WHAT IS IT YOU FIND TO *DO* BACK THERE ALL DAY?

THIS AND THAT, MR. BEAST.

THIS AND THAT.

SHE'S A **STRANGE** OLD DUCK, ISN'T SHE?

WHAT HAVE YOU FOUND OUT ABOUT **BOY BLUE,** SHERIFF?

WELL, I'M STILL CONDUCTING MY INVESTIGA-TION.

YOU'VE HAD **MONTHS.** TELL ME WHAT YOU KNOW SO FAR.

WHAT I CAN **PROVE** IS THIS: BLUE STOLE THE **WITCHING CLOAK,** THE **VORPAL SWORD** AND **PINOCCHIO'S** BODY.

TO **HELL** WITH WORK. I NEED SOME EXERCISE. **WALK** WITH ME.

WHAT I **SUSPECT** IS THIS: HE'S GONE BACK TO THE HOMELANDS TO DELIVER PINOCCHIO TO **GEPETTO,** IN RE-TURN FOR GEPETTO'S HELP IN FREEING RED RIDING HOOD-- THE **REAL** ONE THIS TIME.

THIS WITCHING CLOAK CAN GET HIM BACK TO THE **HOMELANDS** WITHOUT AN OPEN GATE?

WE THINK SO. IT'S A VERY POWERFUL DEVICE. AFTER CENTURIES WE STILL HAVEN'T WORKED OUT **EVERYTHING** IT CAN DO.

DON'T WE HAVE SOME KIND OF ONGOING **PROGRAM** WHERE INDIVIDUAL FABLES ARE ASSIGNED DIFFERENT MAGIC THINGS TO **PRACTICE** WITH?

SO THAT WE BECOME PROFICIENT IN ACTUALLY **USING** ALL THIS **JUNK** WE SPIRITED OUT OF THE HOMELANDS?

DIDN'T I READ SOMETHING LIKE THAT, IN ONE OF THOSE PILES OF *CRAP* I'VE BEEN WADING THROUGH?

YES, SIR. IT'S CALLED THE *ARTIFACT FAMILIARIZATION PROGRAM.* I BELIEVE I SAW THE FILE SOMEWHERE ON YOUR DESK LAST WEEK.

FINE. SO LET'S GET WHOEVER IT IS WE ASSIGNED TO TRAIN WITH THE WITCHING CLOAK *IN* HERE, AND FIND OUT *EXACTLY* WHAT IT CAN DO.

NO, WAIT. DON'T *TELL* ME.

IT WAS *BLUE?*

YES, SIR. SINCE HE SUCCESSFULLY USED THE THING TO ESCAPE THE HOMELANDS, IT WAS ONLY *NATURAL* HE'D BE THE ONE ASSIGNED TO EXPLORE ITS FULL CAPABILITIES.

LOVELY. JUST *LOVELY.*

AS LONG AS I'M PILING ON THE BAD NEWS, I'D BETTER TELL YOU ABOUT THE *OTHER* MATTER.

WHAT *NOW?* RIOTS AT THE *FARM?* *CANNNIBALISM* ABOVE THE CANDY STORE?

SO FAR WE'VE DIS- COVERED THIRTY-SIX SEPARATE *TREASURE ROOMS* IN BLUE- BEARD'S APART- MENT.

WITH NO INDICATION THAT WE'VE FOUND THEM ALL YET. *GLORIOUS,* ISN'T IT?

SO WHAT'S THE PROBLEM?

THE LATEST INVENTORY ACCOUNTS FOR ONLY *THIRTY-FIVE* ROOMS FULL OF LOOT.

SOMEONE *STOLE* ONE OF MY TREASURE ROOMS?

ERR... ONE OF *OUR* TREASURE ROOMS?

WELL, THE *ROOM'S* STILL THERE, BUT--

DON'T GET *CUTE*, BEAST. HOW MUCH IS MISSING AND WHERE *IS* IT?

IT COULD JUST BE AN *ACCOUNTING* MISTAKE, SIR. WE WERE MOVING THE LOOT ALL OVER THE PLACE, JUST BEFORE THE *BATTLE* LAST YEAR.

HOW MUCH?

DEPENDING ON MARKET CONDITIONS AND THE COST OF CONVERTING IT TO UNTRACEABLE CAPITAL--

HOW MUCH?

BETWEEN TWO-POINT-FOUR AND SIX *BILLION.*

BILLION? WITH A **"B"?**

BLUEBEARD WAS VERY **RICH,** SIR.

I SUSPECT **JACK.** HE LEFT TOWN LAST FALL, AND--

SO DID **BIGBY** AND **SNOW** AND **BLUE** AND HALF A DOZEN **OTHERS!**

FABLES SEEM TO BE **LEAVING TOWN** RIGHT AND LEFT!

TRUE, BUT BIGBY ADVISED ME TO ALWAYS SUSPECT JACK **FIRST.**

DAYS PASS, GETTING COLDER AS THEY ACCUMU-LATE.

WHO **IS** THAT? WHO'S **THERE?**

I **KNOW** SOMEONE'S OUT HERE!

YOU CAN'T FOOL **ME,** NO SIR!

DAMN KIDS, WITH YOUR **PRANKS** AND RASCALLY WAYS!

WHAT? WHAT ARE YOU--? STOP THAT!

H-H-H- =GASP!=

HELP! I'M--

=ACCC-CKKK!=

PLEASE-- STOP-- PLEASE-- DON'T--KILL--

We should take one of the trucks and drive down to the city and DEMAND our transformations from that nasty BASTARD!

You SHOULDN'T ought to talk about the MAYOR that way. He'll come through. Handsome princes ALWAYS come through in the end.

What could POSSIBLY make you believe THAT?

It's in ALL the storybooks.

Should I STEP IN, ROSE?

No, it's just a harmless GRIPE session.

Let 'em blow off some STEAM.

GOO, GOO, GA, GA! *GOO, GOO, GA, GA!*

SAY *MAMA!* SAY *DADA!*

SAY *SHITFIRE* AND DAMNATION!

STOP IT. DON'T TEACH MY KIDS *BAD WORDS.*

HAVEN'T THE BABIES BEEN OUT IN THE *COLD* A LONG TIME, SNOW?

OH, HI ROSE.

THEY DON'T SEEM TO MIND THE COLD AT *ALL.*

IN FACT, I DON'T REALLY NEED TO BUNDLE THEM UP SO *WARM,* BUT HOW WOULD I LOOK IF I *DIDN'T?*

WHAT ARE YOU DOING?

CATCHING UP ON *OLD* MAIL.

WHY SO *GLUM?* MISSED YOUR CHANCE AT THE PUBLISHERS CLEARING-HOUSE SWEEPSTAKES?

LOOK AT *THIS.* IT'S FROM *FRAU TOTEN-KINDER.*

Dear Snow,
Congratulations on the birth of your fine, healthy babies. But I caution you not to automatically assume that seven children is always a lucky number.

Totenkinder

SEVEN?

BUT I HAD *SIX* CHILDREN.

I WONDER HOW SHE COULD GET *THAT* WRONG.

BECAUSE SHE'S A DOTTY OLD *HAG.* LIFE'S TOO *SHORT* TO LET SHIT LIKE THIS WORRY YOU.

COME IN AND GET SOME *HOT COCOA* WHILE YOUR MUNCH-KINS PLAY.

DON'T LET THEM FLOAT TOO *FAR,* BOYS!

TEN MINUTES *ONLY,* AND THEN HAUL THEM STRAIGHT *HOME!*

I *MEAN* IT THIS TIME!

YOOP!

AND NONE OF *THAT!*

NO MORE DRAGGING THEM THROUGH THE SKY AT A MILLION MILES AN HOUR!

EVEN THOUGH THEY *LOVE* IT!

MEANWHILE...

WHO FOUND THE BODY?

MISS MUFFET FOUND HIM.

SHE WAS HEADING OUT TO OPEN THEIR MARKET WHEN SHE DISCOVERED **WEB** HERE JUST OUTSIDE THEIR DOOR.

LET ME GO! **LET ME GO!** I HAVE TO **HELP** HIM!

NOW, **NOW**, MRS. WEB. THERE'S NOTHING MORE YOU CAN DO.

ANY CON-CLUSIONS YET, DOC-TOR?

HE DIED OF **SUFFOCATION.** BUT HIS TRACHEA WASN'T COLLAPSED.

THERE'RE NO LIGATURE MARKS ON HIS NECK, NOR BRUISING AROUND HIS MOUTH AND NOSE.

NOTHING TO INDICATE **FORCIBLE BLOCKING** OF HIS AIRWAY.

SO THIS WAS FROM **NATURAL CAUSES?** IT WASN'T MURDER?

I'M NOT RULING ANYTHING **OUT**, UNTIL I CAN DO AN AUTOPSY.

TRUTH IS, I HAVE **NO** IDEA HOW HE DIED.

DAYS LATER, AND THE WINTER GROWS DARKER.

ANY NEWS ABOUT MR. WEB?

NOTHING NEW. APPARENTLY DR. SWINE-HEART'S AUTOPSY WAS *INCONCLUSIVE,* WHICH IS MEDICAL-SPEAK FOR "WE DON'T KNOW ANYTHING."

BUT AT LEAST I HAVE SOME GOOD NEWS FOR *YOU.*

GRAB A PEW, FLYCATCHER.

I'VE BEEN GOING THROUGH BIGBY'S RECORDS. *THIS* MONSTER IS YOUR FILE.

I'VE COMMITTED A *LOT* OF CRIMES.

MINOR VIOLATIONS. I WOULDN'T CALL *ANY* OF THEM CRIMES.

AND THAT'S WHAT I WANT TO TALK TO YOU ABOUT. BIGBY'S HAD YOU DOING COMMUNITY SERVICE FOR *YEARS*-- YEARS OF PUNISH-MENT FOR THE *TINIEST* INFRAC-TIONS.

AS NEAR AS I CAN TELL, HE WAS USING YOUR ODD EATING HABITS AS AN *EXCUSE* TO EXTORT A LIFETIME OF JANITORIAL AND MAINTENANCE *SERVICE* FROM YOU.

I FIND THAT *DESPICABLE.*

BUT--

SO, AS OF THIS MINUTE, I'M DECLARING ALL DEBTS *PAID.* YOU DON'T OWE US ANOTHER MINUTE'S WORTH OF WORK.

CONGRATU-LATIONS, FLY. YOU'RE FREE TO *GO.*

BUT--

DON'T WORRY, BUDDY. I'M PREPARED TO LOOK THE OTHER WAY AT ANY NEW INFRACTIONS.

YOU DON'T HAVE TO WORRY ABOUT ME HAULING YOU BACK IN HERE--NOT *EVER.*

BUT--

AND NO MORE LIVING ON A COT IN A CORNER OF THE BOILER ROOM. I'VE ALREADY PUT YOUR NAME ON THE WAITING LIST FOR A FABLETOWN APARTMENT.

I DON'T KNOW IF WE CAN GET YOU INTO THE *WOODLAND* HERE, BUT I DEFINITELY THINK WE CAN FIND YOU A PLACE SOMEWHERE ON BULLFINCH STREET.

I'M THE SHERIFF, AFTER ALL. AND WHAT'S *THAT* WORTH IF I CAN'T PULL A FEW STRINGS FOR SOMEONE WHO'S SERVED THE COMMUNITY SO WELL, FOR SO LONG?

BUT--

A BIT OVERWHELMING, ISN'T IT?

I DON'T KNOW *WHY* BIGBY SEEMED TO HAVE SUCH A HUGE PERSONAL NUT AGAINST YOU, BUT I DON'T WORK THAT WAY.

I THINK YOU'LL FIND MY STYLE TO BE QUITE DIFFERENT--A LOT LESS *OPPRESSIVE* THAN MY PREDECESSOR.

I'LL BET YOU'LL BE GLAD TO FINALLY GET OUT OF THAT ORANGE *JUMPSUIT,* EH, BIG GUY?

AND CHECK BACK *IN* WITH ME IN A FEW DAYS TO LET ME KNOW HOW YOU'RE *DOING.*

THAT'S NOT AN *ORDER.* IT'S AN INVITATION.

AND HEY, BUDDY, DON'T OVERDO THE *CELEBRATING* TONIGHT. I'D HATE TO START YOUR NEW EMANCIPATION BY HAVING TO HAUL YOU IN FOR PUBLIC *DRUNKENNESS.*

JUST *KIDDING,* FLY. YOU ENJOY YOUR LIBERATION.

...HOMELESS...

H'LO, FLY? HOW'S IT HANGING?

...I DON'T KNOW WHERE TO GO...

SO MUCH FREE TIME YOU CAN'T DECIDE WHAT TO DO WITH IT? I *ENVY* YOU, MAN.

MISS WHITE! MISS RED! COME QUICK!

WHAT THE HELL'S GOING ON OUT HERE?

QUIET! I JUST PUT THE KIDS DOWN!

SOMEONE'S COME!

STRANGERS!

AN INVASION!

CLARA, WATCH THE BABIES!

GUARD THEM!

WHAT NOW?

ISN'T ONE DAMNED THING, IT'S ANOTHER!

GREETINGS, FABLES IN EXILE.

SPRING HAS ARRIVED.

BRIGHT.

BLUSTERY.

AND BREEZY.

UNTIL THE SPRING

In which bodies accumulate, the sheriff gets a good scolding, war is discussed and a pack of floaters celebrate their first birthday.

YOU SHOULDN'T LET THEM FLY ABOUT LIKE THAT, SNOW.

HOW COULD I *STOP* THEM, MR. NORTH? THEY LOVE IT. THEY *LIVE* FOR IT.

THEY'RE *NOT* ORDINARY CHILDREN.

BELIEVE ME, MR. NORTH, I NOTICED.

WE'RE *FAMILY*, SNOW. YOU DON'T HAVE TO BE SO FORMAL. YOU CAN EVEN CALL ME "DAD" IF YOU LIKE.

THAT'S NOT EXACTLY *APPROPRIATE* THOUGH, SINCE I'M NOT *MARRIED* TO YOUR SON.

SO YOU KEEP REMINDING ME WITHOUT EVER EXPLAINING *WHY*.

IT'S *COMPLI-CATED*.

ANOTHER THING YOU REPEAT OFTEN.

BUT, TO RETURN TO THE SUBJECT, YOU HAVE *EXTRAORDINARY* CHILDREN WHO'RE GOING TO NEED EXTRAORDINARY *TRAINING*.

THEY'RE LEARNING TO *FLY* BUT NOT *WALK*. THEY AREN'T *TALKING* YET AND HALF OF THEM STILL LOOK *INHUMAN*.

SO WHAT AM I SUPPOSED TO *DO* ABOUT THAT? THEY WERE *BORN* THAT WAY.

TEACH THEM TO *SHAPESHIFT*, OF COURSE. IF YOU WAIT TOO LONG, THEY WON'T BE *ABLE* TO LEARN IT.

BIGBY REFUSED TO BE ANYTHING BUT A *WOLF*, SINCE HE NEVER MUCH CARED FOR ME, AND TOOK MORE TO HIS MOTHER.

3 pigs

BEFORE LONG IT WAS TOO *LATE*. HE WAS *STUCK* IN ONE SHAPE-- UNTIL *YOU* CAME ALONG, CENTURIES LATER WITH THAT LYCANTHROPY- STAINED KNIFE.

MY GRAND- CHILDREN SHOULD'VE AT LEAST LEARNED TO CHANGE BETWEEN THEIR BASIC *HUMAN* AND *WOLF* FORMS BY NOW.

THE THINGS YOU SAY-- THEY *ASTONISH* ME.

THEY'RE STILL A WEEK AWAY FROM THEIR *FIRST* BIRTHDAY.

AND WHY AREN'T THEY *TALKING* YET?

RIGHT. TIME'S SLIPPING BY. THEY SHOULDV'E BEEN TALKING BY THEIR SECOND *MONTH*.

WHAT'S THAT COMMOTION UP THERE?

Blacks...

REYNARD, WHAT'S THAT CROWD DOING IN THE SQUARE?

MARY'S LITTLE LAMB *DIED*. FOUND IT EARLY THIS MORNING. EVERYONE KNOWS. WHERE'VE YOU *BEEN* ALL DAY, SNOW BUNNY?

WALK- ING IN THE WOODS.

LET'S GO SEE WHAT *HAPPENED*.

HE'S JUST LIKE THE OTHER FOUR. *SUFFOCATED* WITH NO SIGNS OF TRAUMA.

FIRST MR. WEB. THEN SALLY MORRISON, BARBARA ALLEN, JACK SPRATT, AND NOW *THIS*.

MARY, YOU CAN TAKE YOUR LAMB *HOME* NOW. AN AUTOPSY WON'T BE NECESSARY.

THERE'S *NOTHING* I CAN LEARN FROM IT.

NOTHING THAT WILL POINT TO *WHO'S* DOING THIS.

SO IT DEFINITELY IS *MURDER* THEN?

IT'S A *WILD* ZEPHYR.

EXCUSE ME?

THE *KILLER* IS A ZEPHYR--A LIVING GUST OF WIND, MUCH LIKE MY ATTENDANT WINDS, EXCEPT THIS *CAN'T* TAKE SOLID FORM.

INVISIBLE?

QUITE SO. YES.

AH--IT BEGINS TO MAKE SENSE.

BUT *WHY* KILL? HOW DOES IT--?

THEY'RE *FOUL,* WILD THINGS. NOT MUCH MORE THAN *BEASTS.*

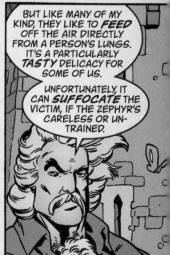

BUT LIKE MANY OF MY KIND, THEY LIKE TO *FEED* OFF THE AIR DIRECTLY FROM A PERSON'S LUNGS. IT'S A PARTICULARLY *TASTY* DELICACY FOR SOME OF US.

UNFORTUNATELY, IT CAN *SUFFOCATE* THE VICTIM, IF THE ZEPHYR'S CARELESS OR UN-TRAINED.

THIS ONE SEEMS NOT TO KNOW, OR NOT TO CARE, ABOUT THE *MORTAL* RESULTS OF ITS FEEDING FRENZIES.

WHY HAVE I *NEVER* HEARD OF SUCH A CREATURE?

THEY'RE *RARE*--A CORRUPTED VERSION OF MY KIND. SOMETHING OF AN EXTREME *BIRTH DEFECT,* ACTUALLY, WHICH WE TEND TO KILL AT NATIVITY.

BUT SOME DO *SLIP* THROUGH THE NET.

I'M SURPRISED ONE COULD EVEN COME TO *EXIST* IN THIS MUNDANE WORLD.

UNLESS IT CAME HERE ALONG *WITH* YOU.

EXCEPT THE *FIRST* VICTIM WAS KILLED WEEKS *BEFORE* MR. NORTH ARRIVED.

ASSUMING HE ACTUALLY *ARRIVED* IN OUR WORLD WHEN HE SAID HE DID.

ONE *OTHER* POSSIBILITY WE SHOULD CON- SIDER.

IT'S BEEN MORE THAN A YEAR SINCE THE ADVERSARY'S WOODEN SOLDIER INVASION--WITH *NO* RESPONSE FROM US.

WHO'S TO SAY HE ISN'T *STRIKING* AGAIN--MORE SUBTLY THIS TIME, BY SENDING THE PERFECT *INVISIBLE* ASSASSIN?

THAT'S POSSIBLE.

WE SHOULD'VE STRUCK BACK *IMMEDIATELY* AFTER THE BATTLE OF FABLETOWN.

WE SHOULD'VE MADE THE ADVERSARY *PAY* A DEAR PRICE FOR HIS DANGEROUS ANTICS-- BLOODIED HIS NOSE SO HE'D *HESITATE* TO DO IT AGAIN.

THE FIRST *KILLINGS* WERE IN FABLETOWN. NOW IT'S MOVED UP TO THE FARM.

IT FITS.

SHERIFF, STAY HERE. FIND A WAY TO CAPTURE THIS THING AND *KILL* IT.

WHERE ARE *YOU* GOING?

BACK TO FABLETOWN TO CONVENE A *WAR* COUNCIL AND DRAFT A PLAN TO STRIKE BACK AT THE HOMELANDS.

KEEP ME POSTED.

HOW DO I KILL A *BREEZE?*

I'LL HELP YOU. NOW THAT I KNOW TO LOOK FOR IT, IT CAN'T LONG ESCAPE DETECTION.

MISTRAL, WHIFF, SQUALL, TRACK THE THING AND *SNUFF* IT.

THIS PLACE IS A MESS!

IT'S TURNING INTO AN ABSOLUTE *PIGSTY!*

I USED TO BE ABLE TO SEE MYSELF IN THE *SHINE* ON THESE FLOORS.

NOW THE TILE LOOKS BROWN AND DINGY.

DON'T *BLAME* ME, MISS BEAUTY. *I'M* NOT THE ONE WHO LIBERATED OUR CUSTODIAN THREE MONTHS BACK.

I GUESS I'M LUCKY I CAN'T SEE ANYTHING.

WHO *ARE* YOU AND WHY ARE YOU HANGING AROUND HERE?

I HAVE AN APPOINTMENT WITH YOUR HUSBAND TODAY, MISS BEAUTY.

WELL, THAT'S *OFF.* HE GOT CALLED AWAY THIS MORNING TO SOME *EMERGENCY* UP AT THE FARM.

GO HOME, KAY, BEFORE SOMEONE *TRIPS* OVER YOU.

GRIMBLE, FIND SOMEONE TO *MUCK* THIS PLACE OUT!

COME WITH *ME*, BABIES.

COME WITH MOMMY.

LET'S GO SEE *GRANDPA*.

MR. NORTH, MAY I TALK TO YOU FOR A MOMENT?

OF COURSE YOU MAY, SNOW. ANY TIME YOU LIKE.

GOOD. I CONSIDERED WHAT YOU TOLD ME EARLIER AND DECIDED YOU'RE *RIGHT*. I WANT YOU TO TRAIN MY BABIES IN THE NATURAL GIFTS OF THEIR HERITAGE.

I'M GLAD TO HEAR THAT, SNOW. I'LL BEGIN AS SOON AS WE FINISH TRACKING DOWN--

NO, I'D PREFER IT IF YOU STARTED *IMMEDIATELY*.

BUT THIS REALLY ISN'T THE TIME TO--

THIS IS *EXACTLY* THE TIME, SIR. YOU SAID YOURSELF THEY'RE ALREADY *FAR* BEHIND IN ESSENTIAL LESSONS, AND ALREADY IN DANGER OF *LOSING* THESE ABILITIES ENTIRELY.

YES, BUT--

WERE YOU *SERIOUS* IN THIS MATTER, SIR, OR MERELY LOOKING FOR A WAY TO CRITIQUE MY MATERNAL CAPABILITIES--PERHAPS AS *ANOTHER* WAY TO CRITICIZE BIGBY BY PROXY?

OF COURSE I WAS SERIOUS! I'M *ALWAYS* SERIOUS!

GOOD, THEN I'LL GET OUT OF YOUR WAY. DARLINGS, STAY WITH GRANDPA, OKAY?

TRUTH IS I'M *RELIEVED* THEY'LL BE WITH YOU--UNDER YOUR *PROTECTION*--WHILE THIS INVISIBLE KILLER MAY BE LURKING ABOUT.

A MOST PRACTICAL CONSIDERATION, SNOW.

NO, SWEETIE, YOU STAY WITH GRANDPA FOR NOW.

MOMMY WILL FETCH YOU LATER.

HOW'S MARY?

DEVASTATED.

HOW WOULD *YOU* FEEL?

MARY

NOTED. SO STINKY MENTIONED YOU WANTED TO TALK TO ME--ABOUT SOMETHING NOT RELATED TO THE LATEST *MURDER?*

IT CAN WAIT.

I DON'T WANT TO *DISTRACT* YOU FROM YOUR INVESTIGATION.

I'VE GOT *NOTHING* TO DO. EITHER MR. NORTH AND HIS BOYS CAN CATCH IT, OR THEY CAN'T, BUT I CAN'T DO DOODLY-SQUAT TO *HELP* THEM.

SO, WHAT'S UP?

WHY DID YOU *FIRE* FLYCATCHER?

FLYCATCHER? WHY ARE WE SUDDENLY TALKING ABOUT *HIM?*

AND FOR THE RECORD, I DIDN'T FIRE HIM. I SET HIM *FREE.*

BIGBY WAS KEEPING THE POOR SUCKER IN PERPETUAL SERVITUDE.

OF *COURSE* HE WAS! THAT WAS THE WHOLE *PLAN!* DON'T YOU *GET* IT?

DON'T YOU KNOW *ANY-THING?*

APPARENTLY NOT. ENLIGHTEN ME.

FLYCATCHER *LOVES* HIS JOB. HE KEEPS EVERYTHING CLEAN AND WORKING IN THE WOODLAND BUILDING. HE'S *IMPORTANT*, BECAUSE EVERYONE COUNTS ON HIM.

YOU TOOK ALL THAT AWAY FROM HIM.

SO, WE'LL GIVE HIM HIS *JOB* BACK, BUT THIS TIME AT A GOOD WAGE. NOT BY PILING UP COMMUNITY SERVICE HOURS ON HIM BECAUSE OF A RIDICULOUS SERIES OF *MINOR* INFRACTIONS.

NO, NO, NO, THAT'S NOT THE WAY IT WORKS.

IF FLY HAS A JOB HE CAN KEEP OR QUIT AT HIS OWN WHIM, THEN HE *HAS* TO QUIT, SO HE CAN TRY TO GET BACK TO THE HOMELANDS, TO FIND HIS *WIFE* AND *KIDS*.

BUT IF HE'S WORKING OFF A SERIES OF NEVER-ENDING *PUNISHMENT* DETAILS, HE ISN'T ALLOWED TO JUST WALK AWAY, SO HE GETS TO STAY HERE, WITHOUT GUILT, AND BE SAFE AND HAPPY.

DAMN. I DIDN'T THINK OF IT THAT WAY.

I NEVER *KNEW*.

BIGBY HAD IT ALL WORKED OUT, YEARS AGO. DIDN'T HE *TELL* YOU?

He told me to always keep busting fly for eating flies, but never explained *WHY*. I just *ASSUMED* fly was another one of his whipping boys--like jack.

And they let *YOU* be sheriff?

Okay, I'll eat my fair share of humble pie, lady, but don't get *SNOTTY*.

Clara told me that Vulco told her that fly's been living in the *EGGMAN'S* basement.

He earns his cot by cleaning up at night, but during the day he's constantly *ASKING* all the customers if they know of a gate still open to the homelands.

Clara and Vulco?

They're dating. But don't change the subject. You need to march right home and *ARREST* fly again.

I will, as soon as this case is--

Right away! before he *LEAVES*, or does some other stupid thing! you said yourself you're *USELESS* on this case, anyway.

"BIGBY'S GONE.

SNOW'S GONE.

BLUE'S GONE.

JACK'S GONE."

BRANSTOCK TAVERN

"COLE GOT HIMSELF BOUNCED OUT OF OFFICE. IT'S ALL GOING TO *PIECES*, ISN'T IT?"

"*JACK'S* GONE TOO?"

"YEAH. TOOK OFF LAST YEAR. DIDN'T YOU NOTICE HE WASN'T *AROUND* ANYMORE?"

"I JUST *ASSUMED* HE'D GOTTEN CAUGHT DOING ONE OF HIS *SCHEMES*, AND GOT HIMSELF LOCKED AWAY IN THE WOODLAND BASEMENT AGAIN.

NAW, HE *CUT* OUT. SAID FABLETOWN WAS *FINISHED* AND THEN HIT THE ROAD."

"MAYBE JACK'S *RIGHT*. MAYBE FABLETOWN *IS* HEADED FOR THE CRAPPER.

THE NEW MAYOR'S CERTAINLY *SHOWN* HIMSELF TO BE NOT WORTH A TINKER'S DAMN."

"AMEN TO THAT, BROTHER."

I'LL NEED PEOPLE CAPABLE OF **STRATEGIC** THINKING-- ONES I CAN TRUST TO KEEP **SECRETS**.

SO LET YOURSELF INTO BIGBY'S--SORRY, INTO **BEAST'S** OFFICE AND PULL HIS FILES ON THE TOURISTS.

YES YOU DO SO KNOW OF THE TOURISTS, BEAUTY. THEY'RE THOSE THREE **SPIES** THE SHERIFF HAS, WHO KEEP TABS ON ALL THE FABLES LIVING ABROAD.

ACTUALLY, SINCE **I'M** THE GODDAMNED MAYOR NOW, THEY'RE THE THREE SPIES **I** HAVE.

SO LET'S HAUL THEM **HOME** AND PUT THEM TO SOME **REAL** WORK.

THERE SHOULD BE CONTACT NUMBERS FOR EACH OF THEM. HOW SHOULD **I** KNOW? SOMEWHERE IN THEIR FILES.

CALL THEM UP AND **ORDER** EACH OF THEM TO GET ON THE NEXT FLIGHT HOME-- TOURIST CLASS.

YES, BEAUTY, **UNLESS** THEY'RE IN THE MIDDLE OF SOME ABSOLUTELY PRESS-ING BIT OF SKUL-DUGGERY.

Mommy?

I *KNEW* YOU'D COME.

YOU'VE BEEN TRYING TO *FIND* ME, HAVEN'T YOU?

ALL THIS TIME.

ALL *ALONE*.

NOT KNOWING HOW TO *FEED* YOURSELF.

Why'd you leave me, Mommy?

I DIDN'T KNOW.

I THOUGHT I'D ONLY HAD *SIX* CHILDREN.

I'M SO *SORRY.*

WE DIDN'T *SEE* YOU, BABY.

But I found you, Mommy.

Finally found you.

I KNOW, BABY. BUT YOU *CAN'T* STAY.

Why?

BECAUSE THEY'LL KILL YOU WHEN THEY FIND YOU.

LISTEN, YOU CAN'T TAKE AIR DIRECTLY FROM PEOPLE ANY-MORE.

NOT ANIMALS EITHER.

But outside air tastes *bad.*

I KNOW, BABY, BUT YOU HAVE TO PROMISE ME. NO MORE INSIDE AIR.

Then I can stay?

NO. I'M SORRY, BUT THEY STILL WOULDN'T *UNDERSTAND.*

YOU HAVE TO GO FAR AWAY, BABY. FAR, FAR AWAY FROM HERE.

YOU HAVE TO GO FIND YOUR *DADDY* AND TELL HIM WHAT HAPPENED.

HE'LL *KNOW* WHAT TO DO AND HE WON'T LET ANY-ONE *HURT* YOU.

CAN YOU DO THAT, BABY? CAN YOU FIND DADDY?

Sure I can, Mommy. I'm learning real good, but--

AND PROMISE YOU'LL STAY WITH HIM *FOREVER* AND EVER?

I'm *sorry* I was bad, Mommy.

HURRY AND GO, *FAST* AS YOU CAN!

BEFORE THEY CATCH YOU.

LIFE GOES ON.

ONE.... TWO....

HAPPY BIRTHDAY, BABIES!

COME ON, KIDS! COME WITH AUNTIE ROSE!

FLIRT

LET'S SEE WHAT MOMMY MADE FOR YOU!

HAPPY BIRTHDAY, MY LOVELY DARLINGS!

SEVEN BIRTHDAY CAKES, SNOW?

YUP. I'M STARTING A NEW *FAMILY* TRADITION.

WHICH I'LL EXPLAIN TO YOU MESSY LITTLE MONSTERS WHEN YOU'RE OLDER.

NOW LET'S OPEN PRESENTS!

The cruel, hot summer
Led into the long, hard fall,
Becoming the dark, killing winter,
Until spring replenished us all.

— *traditional nursery rhyme*

Look for these other VERTIGO books:
All VERTIGO titles are Suggested for Mature Readers

BARNUM!
Howard Chaykin/David Tischman/
Niko Henrichon

BIGG TIME
Ty Templeton

BLACK ORCHID
Neil Gaiman/Dave McKean

THE COWBOY WALLY SHOW
Kyle Baker

**DEADENDERS: STEALING
THE SUN**
Ed Brubaker/Warren Pleece

**DESTINY: A CHRONICLE OF
DEATHS FORETOLD**
Alisa Kwitney/various

**THE DREAMING: THROUGH THE
GATES OF HORN & IVORY**
Caitlin R. Kiernan/Peter Hogan/
various

ENIGMA
Peter Milligan/Duncan Fegredo

GODDESS
Garth Ennis/Phil Winslade

HEAVY LIQUID
Paul Pope

THE HOUSE ON THE BORDERLAND
Simon Revelstroke/Richard Corben

HOUSE OF SECRETS: FOUNDATION
Steven T. Seagle/Teddy Kristiansen

HOUSE OF SECRETS: FAÇADE
Steven T. Seagle/Teddy Kristiansen

HUMAN TARGET
Peter Milligan/Edvin Biukovic

HUMAN TARGET: FINAL CUT
Peter Milligan/Javier Pulido

HUMAN TARGET: STRIKE ZONES
Peter Milligan/Javier Pulido

I DIE AT MIDNIGHT
Kyle Baker

I, PAPARAZZI
Pat McGreal/Stephen John Phillips/
Steven Parke

**IN THE SHADOW OF EDGAR
ALLAN POE**
Jonathon Scott Fuqua/
Stephen John Phillips/Steven Parke

JONNY DOUBLE
Brian Azzarello/Eduardo Risso

KING DAVID
Kyle Baker

THE LITTLE ENDLESS STORYBOOK
Jill Thompson

THE LOSERS: ANTE UP
Andy Diggle/Jock

**MICHAEL MOORCOCK'S
MULTIVERSE**
Michael Moorcock/Walter Simonson/
Mark Reeve

MR. PUNCH
Neil Gaiman/Dave McKean

THE MYSTERY PLAY
Grant Morrison/Jon J Muth

THE NAMES OF MAGIC
Dylan Horrocks/Richard Case

NEIL GAIMAN & CHARLES VESS' STARDUST
Neil Gaiman/Charles Vess

NEIL GAIMAN'S MIDNIGHT DAYS
Neil Gaiman/Matt Wagner/various

NEVADA
Steve Gerber/Phil Winslade/
Steve Leialoha

ORBITER
Warren Ellis/Colleen Doran

**PREACHER: DEAD OR ALIVE
(THE COLLECTED COVERS)**
Glenn Fabry

PRIDE & JOY
Garth Ennis/John Higgins

PROPOSITION PLAYER
Bill Willingham/Paul Guinan/Ron Randall

**SANDMAN MYSTERY THEATRE:
THE TARANTULA**
Matt Wagner/Guy Davis

**THE SANDMAN PRESENTS:
THE FURIES**
Mike Carey/John Bolton

**THE SANDMAN PRESENTS:
TALLER TALES**
Bill Willingham/various

**SCENE OF THE CRIME: A LITTLE PIECE
OF GOODNIGHT**
Ed Brubaker/Michael Lark/
Sean Phillips

**SHADE, THE CHANGING MAN:
THE AMERICAN SCREAM**
Peter Milligan/Chris Bachalo

SKREEMER
Peter Milligan/Brett Ewins/
Steve Dillon

THE SYSTEM
Peter Kuper

TELL ME, DARK
Karl Wagner/John Ney Rieber/
Kent Williams

TERMINAL CITY
Dean Motter/Michael Lark

TRUE FAITH
Garth Ennis/Warren Pleece

UNCLE SAM
Steve Darnall/Alex Ross

UNDERCOVER GENIE
Kyle Baker

UNKNOWN SOLDIER
Garth Ennis/Kilian Plunkett

V FOR VENDETTA
Alan Moore/David Lloyd

VEILS
Pat McGreal/Stephen John Phillips/
José Villarrubia/Rebecca Guay

WHY I HATE SATURN
Kyle Baker

WITCHCRAFT
James Robinson/Peter Snejbjerg/
Michael Zulli/various

THE WITCHING HOUR
Jeph Loeb/Chris Bachalo/
Art Thibert

YOU ARE HERE
Kyle Baker

Visit us at www.vertigocomics.com for more information on these and many other titles from VERTIGO and DC Comics
or call 1-888-COMIC BOOK for the comics shop nearest you, or go to your local book store.